MW00917524

PROJECT

How to Prioritize Your To-Do List, Pick the Most Important Projects, and Get Them Done

Jackie Hernandez

Cover by Kelsey Baldwin (www.paperandoats.com)
Edited by Janna Madsen (www.jannaemadsen.wix.com/revisions)
Author photograph by Melissa Miroslavich

ISBN: 1515336158
ISBN-13: 978-1515336150

www.TealandLime.com/books

For José, Pepé, and Jax—
my home project team.

PROJECT

FREE GIFT

Creating a home is a journey of self-discovery. There are so many things I wish I had known when I moved into my first home. Now on my third home, I periodically need to be reminded of the same things. To keep my home on track I use seven simple exercises. I've compiled them in this *free* PDF, complete with a worksheet for each exercise. I hope the **Make Your Home Happy Workbook** helps you create a home that looks and works better for you.

Download your workbook here:
http://www.tealandlime.com/home-happy-workbook/

Contents

Introduction

We had a painfully long to-do list and every time a friend hinted at stopping by the house we quickly changed the subject. We used to love hosting friends for dinner, but the vision we had for our kitchen remodel wasn't becoming a reality fast enough.

When we bought our first home, the view of the Chesapeake Bay out the living room windows obviously blinded us to the awful state of the kitchen. When we did our final walk-through just before closing, the ugliness hit us hard. At dinner that night we wondered how we had missed the horrible vinyl floor, peeling laminate counters, or forest green accent tiles when we bought the house. How do you miss that kind of stuff? So we immediately started planning a kitchen makeover. We couldn't afford to gut it, but we knew some cosmetic changes could make a world of difference.

We wanted to paint the cabinets white, install new countertops, and add additional cabinets in an unused corner of the room. We wanted to put down new flooring, change out the appliances, add a microwave over the stove, and about a dozen other things. We were pretty pumped and figured we could just get started and finish in a few weeks, maybe a month at most.

Six months later we were still dodging friends that wanted to hang out at our place and feeling guilty about those who invited us over for dinner when we couldn't return the favor. On one hand, we simply didn't want our friends to see the mess. On the other hand, we were starting to get embarrassed about how long the project was taking.

The problem was that we didn't do any planning. We didn't set a budget, make a schedule, or even decide all the things we wanted to do. We just started ripping out the ugly and making it up as we went along. Nearly a year later, the kitchen turned out fine, but I think we could have saved about nine months if we had planned properly in the beginning. Instead we let our enthusiasm to beautify our new home overshadow everything we knew about effectively managing a project (which was quite a bit, since we were both employed as project managers at the time). We only lived in that home for a year and a half, most of which was spent not having guests over and not truly enjoying our home. Even when we listed the house to sell, there were still projects in the kitchen we wished we had finished, but never got to because of poor planning. It didn't have to be that way.

Is your to-do list managing you instead of the other way around? Do you keep adding on more projects than you knock off? Or do your undone projects have you paralyzed to the point that you're not checking things off the list at all? If you said yes to any of those, then *Project Home* will help.

Decorating, managing, and keeping up your home is a bigger undertaking than you ever imagined. Your home is also a main source of your dreams and goals. You spend a lot of time at home. You raise your family at home. You want to improve your home on an ongoing basis. So naturally, the to-do list seems never-ending.

Like most of the finer things in life—a healthy marriage, raising children, building a career—creating a home doesn't come with an instruction manual. There isn't a blueprint for what to do when and what to do next. It's up to you to figure it out what to do and where to begin.

In this book, my goal is to help you figure out where to focus and how to take back control of your to-do list. I'll show you how to manage your list, so it doesn't manage you. Then, I'll give you the tools you need to get more projects on your home to-do list done. I want to help you find more time for enjoying your home rather than working on it.

I've refined this system over ten years and across the three homes I've owned. During much of that time I worked as a professional project manager for software development projects. I translated many of the things that made my projects successful at work to successful projects at home.

In Part One of this book, we'll cover how to get and stay motivated to meet your home goals, what really causes your home projects to fail, and how to better plan your way to success. Then, I'll give you a process for cleaning up your to-do list, so you can focus on the most important projects. I'll share with you the exact four-step system I use for figuring out what *is* important—those home projects that will have the biggest impact on your quality of life. A by-product of the to-do list cleanup is a separate list of projects you shouldn't do because those projects won't be worth your time, money, or energy.

In Part Two, I'll teach you just enough project management to be useful around the house: how to manage the scope of your project (what's included and what's not), how to create a schedule (when you'll get it done), and how to use a budget (how much it will cost). While motivation and focus are good enough to get you started, project management is what will help you finish. If you follow along and take action, by the end of this book you'll have a project plan for your most important project.

Throughout the book I will share additional resources in the form of online bonuses, including worksheets and videos illustrating key concepts. You can access all the bonuses in a single bundle here:

Online Bonus
Download all the *Project Home* bonuses here:
www.TealandLime.com/ProjectHomeBonus

If you follow the process in this book, you'll know exactly where to focus in your home so you can spend your time on the most worthwhile projects. You'll also learn how to successfully manage your projects so they get happily crossed off the list and you can get back to enjoying your home.

PART ONE

Motivation and Focus

By the end of the first half of this book, you'll have a prioritized and ranked home project list so you know exactly which project you should tackle next. But first we need to get the mindset stuff out of the way. The real reason your to-do list is never-ending probably has to do with motivation and focus. I know you're eager to make some progress in your home so you may want to jump right to the section on focus, but it won't do you any good unless you are first motivated to tackle some of your home projects. I'm not just talking about big home projects, like renovations, either. Everything on your to-do list is really a project, big or small. All the things you want to do, from rearranging the furniture to planting roses in the garden, are projects. To get more stuff done around the house, you need a little project motivation.

The best projects are the finished ones, but there are three other types of projects we need to talk about here:

1. Unfinished projects
2. Unstarted projects
3. Finished, but failed projects

I'm certain you've experienced all three and each type takes a toll on your overall motivation and confidence to move forward in your home. I have some specific strategies to deal with each of these types of project failure so you'll have the drive you need to complete the next project you focus on.

CHAPTER ONE

How to Finish a Long Overdue Project

Let's begin with the projects you were motivated to start, but not motivated to finish. We've all got one of those undone projects. This project isn't just an idea in your head; it's a half-done eyesore you've been putting up with forever. But for some reason it seems easier to ignore than to finish.

You come up with every possible excuse. Some of them are pretty convincing. Meanwhile, it takes up space in your mind, keeping you from truly relaxing in your home. You think about it a lot. *Will it ever get done? Is it even worth finishing? Should I just scrap it and start over? Maybe we just need to move.*

Everyone gets stuck. Sometimes projects take longer than expected or turn out harder than you thought. Sometimes life just gets in the way of finishing projects. The longer the project sits half-done, the longer it takes you to get back to it. Unfinished almost becomes acceptable.

Once you've stopped working on a project, it gets harder to pick it up again. It's project inertia. A project at rest tends to stay at rest, while a project in motion tends to stay in motion. In this chapter, we'll talk about how to find the motivation to get started again and how to keep up the momentum to finish.

I get stuck, too. I am a planner through and through. I tend to finish what I start, more often than not. There was one project that got the better of me, though. Friends and family know that for almost two years, our two-story living room walls were half-painted. Not like "one coat of paint" half-painted, but rather "one color on the bottom and another color on the top" half-painted. The last time my husband and I worked on it we ran out of paint and never got back to it. We left roller marks halfway up the wall. One weekend two years later, we finally spent about eight hours over the course of two days finishing the room.

But why did it take us nearly two years to finish painting a room?

We love painting, but we are both a little scared of heights (me more than my husband). We didn't want to hire a painter (we never have and probably never will, because it's one job we like to do ourselves). We didn't want to rent scaffolding (when you're scared of heights, rickety metal scaffolding doesn't sound any better). We made valiant efforts to paint the room, but we gave up at 75 percent. We chickened out when it came time to trim around the second floor windows and cut in the wall next to the 17 ft.-high white ceiling. If we bumped the ceiling with the roller or did a bad trim job, we'd mess up the ceiling (which we could barely reach).

So we froze. We didn't finish. We used every excuse in the book, many totally valid, but none of them were the real reasons we weren't moving forward. *We have full-time jobs. We have small kids. We're out of paint. They discontinued the base paint. Now, they discontinued the paint color. Our ladder isn't tall enough. It's too dark to paint at night after the kids are in bed.* I could keep going, because there are a million ways we justified this half-done project.

Thankfully, we stopped apologizing for the state of the room years ago. I even hosted my sister-in-law's baby shower with half-painted walls, putting streamers and balloons at the demarcation line hoping no one would notice. Our friends and family just stopped asking about it. (By the way, none of them offered to babysit or help so we could get it done either!) So, it just became the elephant in the room.

At some point all of our excuses ran out. After years of living in a half-painted room, there were no external stimuli that motivated us to get it done, so instead we had to find our own internal motivation. When we found out the paint color was discontinued, we went and bought the few gallons they had left in stock. The paint still sat there taunting us for a couple of weeks. The old tan color of the walls stared down upon us from the top of the room. It was finally time.

Two years later and the biggest fear holding us back (accidentally painting the ceiling) never came true.

How to Follow Through

It's normal to get stuck, but it's really no fun to live in a home full of half-done projects. I don't want you to wait as long as I did to get your project done.

Keep an Eye on the Big Picture

It got too easy for us to just not look up anymore (literally) and pretend the room was done. We lost sight of how amazing the finished result would be.

Try using an inspiration picture to remind yourself of the

end goal. It's easy to ignore or hide an unsightly half-done project; it's harder to avert your eyes from the beautiful inspiration picture you want to create in your home.

Figure Out Why You're Procrastinating

If it were as simple as running out of time, you would have found more. If you thought it was too hard to DIY, you would have hired someone to do it. So, what's the real reason you aren't finishing?

We made up a lot of excuses, but the truth was we were just scared to cut in around the ceiling. We let that four-inch strip of wall touching the pristine white ceiling hold us back from painting the other seventeen feet.

Procrastination can be a symptom of being a perfection-ist. It's classic perfection paralysis—not finishing, because you worry it won't be perfect. In the end, I realized living in a sloppy half-painted room was much less perfect than a fully painted room with possible ceiling touch-ups required.

If you're not a perfectionist, procrastination might be a sign you're afraid of failure—a fear that the task is too big or unfamiliar and you might not be up to the task. You won't know until you try. We ultimately decided to give painting the second story of the room a try, knowing if it didn't work out we could hire a professional painter to come fix it. By resigning to that worst-case scenario—and making a Plan B— we freed ourselves from the fear of not being good enough. We decided to try our best.

Choose a Deadline and Enough Time

Ever notice things never seem to get done when there is no deadline? Parkinson's Law states, "Work expands so as to fill the time available for its completion." That means with-out a deadline your project will never get done. *Always* put

MY TRUTH

yourself on a deadline, with a realistic plan that includes enough time to complete the entire project. If it's a big project, add some buffer time to the plan.

Although we finally found the internal motivation to finish our living room, an impending visit from my in-laws became the deadline. I could have given myself a deadline much sooner. It was ridiculous that it went two years between attempts to paint this room. When we finally got back to it, the paint color wasn't a match, so we ended up repainting the entire space top to bottom. It was more work in the end, because we didn't follow through from the start.

Don't Delay

A project that is still an idea floating around in your head is one thing; having a project you physically started but never finished is another. Living in a half-done space starts to feel like living a half-baked life.

No matter how much I cleaned the living room, it still looked like a mess. I overcompensated for its undone-ness when all along I should have focused on how to get it done. Instead, we lived for two years in a half-done room that only took eight hours of work to finish. Now, I can finally sit in the room without thinking, "Oh yeah, I still need to do that, too."

The finished room is a night-and-day difference. It doesn't feel like a sloppy mess that I prefer not to talk about. It's no longer the running inside joke amongst family and friends who probably had bets on when we'd finish it. The finished room is beautiful, top to bottom. It makes the whole space feel clean and put together.

When you finally finish that undone project, you'll say, "What took me so long?! I should have done this two years ago." So, what are you waiting for? Get the big picture in your sights, find the root of your procrastination, and tackle it with a firm deadline.

TAKEAWAYS

- Undone projects cause undue stress. It's hard to fully relax in a half-done space.
- Follow through requires figuring out the root of your procrastination first. Why are you really stalling?
- Give yourself a deadline with a reasonable amount of time to finish. When you're done, you'll wonder why you didn't tackle it sooner.

While finishing half-done projects is important, your list of projects to finish up is probably a lot shorter than the list of projects you haven't started yet. They might be ideas, dreams, or a line on your to-do list. You can't find the time, money, or energy to even get them started. That's also a motivation problem. In the next chapter, I'll share eleven ways to get motivated and stay motivated to start and finish more projects.

CHAPTER TWO

Get More Projects Done

I know it's hard to find time for decorating and home improvement. Some projects feel so big that if you don't have a lot of time, it doesn't seem worth starting something you can't finish. You certainly don't want another half-done project on your hands, but at the same time you won't reach your home goals without taking action. You have to start somewhere.

You might be envious of the people you think have it all together and seem to get everything done. Know this: They're not getting it all done. They might be getting some very visible top priorities done and it's likely you're not seeing the chaos, help, time, or money spent behind the scenes. Chances are they, too, have undone and unstarted projects. If they don't, they've likely mastered some, if not all, of the strategies below.

The secret to getting it all done is knowing how to get the most important things done first and not putting anything else on the list. These eleven strategies will help you find and maintain the momentum to tackle your top priorities.

1. Set Attainable and Specific Goals

Be very clear about what you want to do and set realistic goals. There are two keys for setting goals and staying motivated: clarity and attainability. Your confidence will skyrocket if you know exactly what you want to do and if you're realistic about what it will take to get it done. At the end of Part One, I'll walk you through my four-step system for figuring out which project you should do first, which project you should tackle next, and which is next after that.

2. Keep Inspiration Front and Center

Are you dreaming of tearing down that wall between your kitchen and living room? Tape an inspiration picture right on the wall as a daily reminder. Every time you see it, it will remind you of the bigger picture and inspire you to plan and save to make that project happen. It's sort of like taping a picture of yourself twenty pounds lighter to your bathroom mirror when you want to lose weight. Imagery and reminders are very powerful motivators.

3. Pencil It In

Nothing is more demotivating than feeling like you don't have enough time for a task. For the projects you really want to complete, you need to find the time. Book an appointment with yourself to get the project started.

There's nothing wrong with starting a project spontaneously, but when the spontaneity wears off you'll be glad you penciled in time to finish the project. Guard that time like you would any other important appointment on your calendar.

4. Rinse and Repeat

You need to make project time a habit. On Saturday mornings, one hour on Wednesday evening...whatever works for you. It's like a regular date night in a long-term monogamous relationship...every Saturday night guaranteed with three backup babysitters on call. (A girl can dream, right?)

Seriously, make planning and executing home projects a priority and a habit. Even if you can only spare fifteen minutes a week, you should get started. If you wait to have all the time you need, you will never get anywhere.

Once you start seeing how much you can accomplish with regular devoted time, you will be more motivated to continue. You also might find yourself motivated to carve out even more time to make progress.

Making project time a habit is also very important for the mundane tasks you don't want to do, but need to do. The daunting task of replacing burned out light bulbs or cleaning out the pantry will be less overwhelming if you have the time set aside.

5. Remove Distractions or At Least Don't Compete with Them

You know the struggle when you're trying to get something done and a little one is tugging at your shirttails? Sometimes you just need to arrange for childcare or a babysitter in order to get focused project time. It's tough, but necessary to get things done.

If you're looking for your spouse to help, don't battle with their prior commitments. If your hubby is a football fan, don't plan to do a project, or expect his help, during the big game. Battling his distraction is more likely to hinder than help the project.

6. Get Your Resources in Order

When you do have precious time to tackle a project, make sure you are ready to go. My number one motivation killer, especially in the winter, is discovering I am out of screws and can't move forward without them. An unplanned trip to the hardware store makes everything grind to a halt.

Make sure you have the tools and supplies you need on hand when project time rolls around. This might mean using one chunk of work time to gather supplies, then waiting for the next scheduled time to actually start the project.

7. Make a Plan

Make a schedule, write out goals, create a mood board, or use whatever kind of plan speaks to you. Having a plan—knowing the steps you need to take—makes everything feel more doable. Write it down, refer to it, and tweak it as you go. In Part Two, I'll show you how to create a project plan with the three most important things you need to run a successful project.

A plan is a tool. At the beginning of the project it describes how you're going to get from Point A to Point B. During the project it helps you measure how far you are from Point B, and helps you get back on course if you accidentally end up at Point C. Then when you finally get to Point B it tells you how well you did.

A plan is also a "living" document. It should be updated regularly and modified as necessary throughout your project. Too many otherwise good project managers have failed because of inflexibility. No project plan is ever set in stone, because there are always unknowns. Good planning and re-planning are key to overcoming any obstacles during your project.

8. Share Your Plan

Tell the people closest to you about your project. Share with friends and family that support and encourage you. Share for accountability.

I do lots of projects, but when I am not feeling motivated to complete something, I tell someone about it. I tell my husband, my mom, or my sister. Something about putting it out there makes me more motivated to get it done, because I feel accountable. I want to go back to whomever I told and show them I got it done. Also when I'm unsure about a project or how to get started, sometimes it helps to talk it out and get an outsider's ideas on how to proceed.

9. Celebrate the Little Things Often

Set interim goals to help track project progress and make sure to celebrate each milestone reached. This is especially important for larger projects, but also works on smaller projects. On a small furniture painting project, I might hold off on eating lunch until I get the piece primed. Once it's primed, I celebrate with a lunch break. Afterward, I find myself more motivated to do the next step.

On larger projects the milestones might take longer to reach, but celebrating them is also sweeter. I remember the night we celebrated the new flooring in our basement. We had a professional install the carpet, but I installed the cork flooring. The night it was all done, we went down as a family and literally rolled around on the floor. We enjoyed the cushiony softness of the carpet and let the boys run around for the first time without worrying they'd scrape their knees on concrete. That's how we celebrated!

They don't have to be big, but celebrations along the way help you look forward to the next milestone and keep up momentum.

10. In a World of Instant Gratification...Hold Out

Celebrating interim goals is a must, but sometimes you have to hold back the really good stuff to make sure you don't skip over the hard, not-so-fun stuff. To keep up momentum and stamina through less glamorous parts of a project, delay the fun stuff.

For example, on a complete room makeover that requires new flooring and painting the walls, it's easy to get distracted shopping for accessories *for when the room is done.*

Instead, use the fun stuff, like buying accessories for the room, as your prize for getting the other work done. Don't let yourself do the fun stuff until you've reached a specific milestone or completed other critical tasks.

11. Visualize the Finished Project

While you're holding out for the fun finishing touches, it's important to take a step back every once in a while and remember the big picture. Take a moment to visualize the finished space. Do this regularly until you can actually see the finished project before you.

As we worked on our basement finishing project, we did periodic walk-throughs. When the basement walls were just framed, we walked through and imagined where all the furniture would go. When the drywall was in, we walked through and daydreamed about flooring, window treatments, and painting. Each walk-through was so simple, but so powerful. Imagining the finished space kept us engaged and thirsty for the next step.

TAKEAWAYS

- When preparing to start a project, set attainable and specific goals, keep your project inspiration front and center, pencil in time to get it done, and make working on the project a regular habit until the project is finished.
- During the project, remove distractions, make sure you have the required supplies and resources ready for your precious project time, and follow a plan.
- To keep up the stamina to finish, share your plan with someone who will hold you accountable. Celebrate small successes, use the fun parts of a project as prizes for finishing less glamorous work, and continually visualize the completed project.

Even if you build up your motivation and finish a project or two, there's still one huge motivation killer lurking around the corner: project failure. In the next chapter, learn how to prevent the most common reason for finished projects that are still failures.

CHAPTER THREE

Why Home Projects Fail and How to Prevent It

When you finish a project and it doesn't meet your expectations, it's disheartening and demotivating. The thrill is gone and your motivation to tackle the next project drops significantly. A failed project can ruin your motivation and focus for upcoming projects.

The good news is that a lot of project failures are avoidable. If you can start a project and keep up the energy to finish it, then it deserves to be a success. So why, then, do some projects end with a letdown? Why don't they bring you joy? And why can't you pinpoint what is "off" so you can fix it?

Dissatisfaction at the end of a project happens when the project didn't turn out the way you wanted. Usually it's because you never clarified what you wanted in the first place.

In project management, we call what you want at the end

of the project "success criteria." The early definition of your expected outcome is how you will know if the project was a success or not. You don't decide it at the end; you decide your success criteria at the beginning. That way you know all along what you are aiming for and what it will take to get there.

Imagine this: you want to paint a focal wall in your family room. You buy some paint, spend an afternoon painting, put the room back together, then you stand back...and you hate it. The color you picked makes the room look smaller and it doesn't look good in the afternoon sunlight. Not only do you hate it, but now you have to find time to redo it or stare at it every day, regretting the moment you picked up the paint brush.

PREVENTING THE LETDOWN

Instead, take a few minutes to think about what you really want at the end of your project—why you want to paint a focal wall in the first place and what you do not want to happen if you paint a focal wall.

You want your focal wall to:
- Draw people into the room
- Create a focal point because you don't have a fire-place
- Refresh the room without painting all the walls

You don't want a focal wall to:
- Clash with other colors in the room
- Look too bold
- Make the room feel smaller

In other words, the finished focal wall will refresh the space with a new focal point that draws people in, but doesn't scream, "Look at me!", and doesn't make the room look smaller. Those are your success criteria.

A really powerful way to think of success criteria is to consider this: If your finished project was a failure, what would have gone wrong? In the focal wall example, your wall color would have clashed and been too bold, possibly making the room feel smaller. Your success criteria define the opposite of that—what your project will look and feel like when it's a success.

With those criteria in mind, it's time to plan your project. Simply knowing your success criteria might change which wall you choose to paint and what color you choose to paint. Your success criteria shouldn't drive you away from something you love, but instead help you plan for the challenges you might need to work around to pull your idea off.

- If you want to draw people into the room, then you want to paint the wall most visible from the entrance of the room.
- If you don't want people to feel like the wall is in their face, then you probably don't want to choose bright orange paint.
- If you choose a dark wall color that makes the room look smaller, then you know you'll have to adjust for that and hang a large mirror onto that wall to reverse the effect.

Your success criteria guide the project—what you plan to do, how you adjust along the way, and how you feel about the project in the end.

GETTING THE RESULT YOU WANT

Success criteria transcend the stuff we usually worry about in projects, like time and money. It doesn't matter how long it takes, how much you spend, or how much you save if the project doesn't turn out to be a success. If the project fails to meet your expectations, then you might as well not have done it. Success criteria get to the heart of why you are doing the project and help you make decisions during the project.

A lot of projects are never finished or don't live up to expectations, because you add and change things on a whim during the project. If you have success criteria, you refer to them before making any changes. How does this thing I want to add, or this thing I want to change, contribute to the success of this project? Does it ensure success or detract from it?

If you are serious about meeting all of your success criteria—getting what you really want—then you should only add or change things only if they are more likely to make the project a success. In Part Two, we'll take a closer look at how to plan success into your project using scope management.

Measuring the Success of Your Project

That regret you feel when a project doesn't live up to your expectations is avoidable. To help prevent the letdown, start with clear, attainable expectations.

It's like shopping for something on Amazon. You want a new camera, read the "most helpful" reviews, and buy one. Then, you're disappointed when it doesn't fit in your purse or come with an adapter to upload pictures to your computer. If you knew those two things were most important to you, then you could have searched reviews discussing those two specific criteria to find a camera that met them.

With your home projects, it's not enough to say, "We're going to makeover the bathroom:

- Paint the walls—check!
- Hang a new mirror—check!
- Replace the shower curtain—check!"

Determining if your project was a success goes beyond checking all the to-dos off the list. It doesn't matter what you checked off if your shared kids' and guest bathroom doesn't look inviting, make your mother-in-law (MIL) feel right at home, and have a place to hide all your kids' bath toys, it's not a success. Expectations should specifically identify how you'll meet your project goal.

Set your success criteria, plan your project to meet them, and check the results of your work against them.

Did the bathroom makeover:

- Lighten up the room and make it look bigger and more inviting?—check!
- Make your MIL compliment how lovely it looks?—check!
- Include hidden, but easily accessible storage for the bath toys?—check!

That's success! Project success can be yours by planning for it upfront.

TAKEAWAYS

- Define clear and specific success criteria—what you really want out of your finished project—to avoid project failure.
- Use your success criteria as a guide throughout the project.
- Measure the success of your project against the criteria you chose.

Now that you know the motivational techniques you can use to avoid project failure, you also need to know how to pick the right projects. More importantly, you need to know which projects shouldn't even be on your list. In the next two chapters, I'll give you the four-step prioritization process that will clean up your to-do list and help you pick the right projects to focus on.

CHAPTER FOUR

Mastering Your Master Project List

There's a lot of satisfaction that comes from crossing things off a list. But if you keep adding to the list at the same time, the satisfaction of crossing one thing off is overshadowed by adding three new things that need to be done.

When you have unfinished projects in your home, they suck up your mental energy. You'll find that you can't relax because you see undone things jumping out at you when you glance around the room. The only way to end the madness is to focus.

The secret to getting it all done is simple: accept that you won't get it all done, and don't even try.

You'll see as you go through the exercises in this chapter and the next that some of the things you really thought you wanted to do may not seem so important anymore. We're going to pull out the most important, impactful projects to focus on and get rid of the rest.

Prioritization is the key to feeling like you're getting it all done. You have to know where to focus first. I use a four-step system to set my home project priorities. The four steps are:

1. The Big Brain Dump
2. Weed Out the Losers
3. Prioritize the Rest
4. Rank the Best

With just those four steps, you'll know what to focus on first and foremost. The best part is this system is fast, so you can use it regularly to refine your list and regain focus.

STEP 1. THE BIG BRAIN DUMP

To properly prioritize all that you want to accomplish in your home, you need to start a master project list. A project doesn't have to be complicated, like building a bed; it could also be painting the bathroom or hanging new curtains in the dining room. Your master project list should include all the projects you need to do and all the projects you want to do. You cannot effectively prioritize your projects until you have a master list of everything.

Make an unedited, unfiltered list—essentially a brain dump—of everything you want to do in your home. Include projects big and small, the ones you should do, the ones you can't wait to do, the ones you think will only get done in your dreams.

When getting started, I think it's helpful to do a walk-through of your home. Look through every room in your home and walk around the exterior to trigger the project list. Use whatever medium you are comfortable with—pen and paper, notes on your phone, a spreadsheet—to capture your list. Ideally, you will maintain this list going forward, but if you ever find yourself overwhelmed and your mind swirling with ideas to do around the house, that's a great time to return to this exercise and make a new list. Get it all out of your head.

Don't do this exercise to drum up projects. Focus on those you already want to do. Get them all captured in one place. It's important to put *all* your project ideas, big and small, through this process. When you have limited time and budget, it is essential to make sure you're prioritizing your projects and focusing on the right ones first.

TAKE ACTION

Write an exhaustive list of all your home project ideas. Be sure to include decorating projects, home improvement projects, and repairs and maintenance.

Online Bonus
Download the *Project Home* Master Project List: www.TealandLime.com/ProjectHomeBonus

STEP 2. WEED OUT THE LOSERS

Once you have your master list, it's time to get real and whittle it down. The goal here is to cut as many loser projects from the list as possible. Projects that never get started or never get done loitering on your to-do list make your entire list seem insurmountable. You have to get rid of the weeds to let the flowers flourish.

Here are five reasons you should cross something off your list right now and never look back:

1. You're just not that into it.
When we first moved into our current home, most of our conversations started with, "Wouldn't it be nice if..." We've since completed a lot of the projects we dreamed of, but we

also scrapped many others. One in particular was a patio in our backyard. *Wouldn't it be nice if there were a patio underneath the deck and we could turn it into a screened porch? Oh, and add an outdoor fireplace, too?* Of course it would be amazing. But when we first thought of it we just had the deck built. With no funds left over after paying for the deck, we would've had to DIY the patio. We weren't into that. Instead, we turned our sights on staining our new deck and making the most of that new outdoor living space. Maybe someday we'll add the patio below.

If you're not motivated to do the project (unless it is a necessary repair), then why is it on your list? Cross off any discretionary projects you're not motivated to do. This includes projects you feel like you're supposed to do (or feel pressured to do by well-meaning family, friends, and neighbors), but aren't interested in and projects you simply won't enjoy doing. Don't leave something on your list just because you think you *should* do it. Limit your list to things you really need and want to do.

2. You can't afford it or won't spend the money on it.

In our second home—a small townhouse—we debated building out a third bedroom in the basement for years. If we split the family room in half we could have created a third bedroom and possibly have made the house work for our growing family a little longer. We knew we didn't have the skills required to do the work, so we got an estimate. This was back in 2009 when the value of our house was already less than we paid for it. So when the contractor's initial estimate to build a wall and closet, which also included some necessary HVAC work, came in north of $7,000, we knew it wasn't the right project for us. I am so glad we finally got an estimate and could stop thinking about it. Had we not gotten serious enough to get the estimate, we wouldn't have ruled out the project and moved on to more important things.

Some projects are definitely worth saving up for, but be honest with yourself. If you're not good at saving up or the project will cost more than you think it's worth, what is the likelihood it will ever happen? Stop pining over things you can't do and get focused on what you can do.

Not sure what you can afford? See the estimating section in Chapter Eleven to get a rough idea of how much your project might cost.

3. It's been on the list for too long.

When we moved furniture into our newly finished basement, I really wanted to reupholster the large sectional sofa. I've tackled a few upholstery jobs in the past and with the straight-line modern sofa, so I knew I could handle the project. I even found the perfect velvet fabric and it would have cost only about $400. I chose the fabric almost exactly two years ago. I never ordered it. I also never scheduled time to recover the sectional. It's clear to me now that it just wasn't that important. Turns out the neutral fabric on the sectional looks good and my boys couldn't care less if they play video games on a tan sectional or a navy blue sectional. I no longer plan to recover it.

If cost, lack of motivation, or something else has caused a project to linger on your to-do list for years, it's time to move on. It's sort of like cleaning out your closet and throwing out everything you have not worn in the last six months, because you'll probably never wear it again. Or if there are boxes you still haven't opened and unpacked six months to a year after moving, odds are, you don't need what's in them. The same goes for projects you claim to want to do, but never start.

Unless you can pinpoint what is going to change to make you get it done, then remove it from the list.

4. You don't have the skills or won't hire it out.

I refused to let our realtor show us our current house. I looked at the pictures online and hated it. You see, I love white kitchen cabinets. I painted the old wood cabinets in our first home a crisp white. For our second home, we sought out white cabinets and white trim. When I first saw a picture of our current kitchen I gagged. It was wood, wood, and more wood. From the maple cinnamon cabinetry to the dark cherry floors to the unfortunate tan walls all I saw was a sea of brown.

Thankfully our realtor persisted and we discovered that this house, even the kitchen, was beautiful in person. But I still wanted to paint the cabinets white. The thing is I'm a perfectionist and in our first home if the cabinets hadn't been in such horrible shape to begin with I wouldn't have been pleased with the quality of my paint job. On these brand new cabinets in a brand new house, I knew my standards would be exceedingly high. I don't have the skills to get the finish I wanted and it's not that important to me to hire it out. Instead, I installed a beautiful, light blue tile backsplash and painted the walls. I love my kitchen now.

If you don't have the skills to complete a project and you're not willing to hire help, then take it off the list. You're better off focusing on the things you can do or are willing to hire out.

5. It's not clearly defined.

Our backyard has a large hill sloping away from the house. For the first two years we lived here, we pondered if we should level the yard, build a retaining wall, or plant trees. It started taking up too much mental energy to mull over all the possibilities. "Do something with the backyard" was too vague. Now after five years of living here, and tackling other more important projects, we've settled on planting a row of birch trees on the bottom of the hill at the end of the yard. It's back on the list, but much clearer this time.

It doesn't have to be crystal clear or fully baked, but vague ideas can leave you spinning your wheels, unable to move forward. A vague idea is not a project in the making; it's a disaster in the making. Take it off the list for now and revisit it once you have more clarity. It doesn't mean it will never happen, but you're clearly not ready to move forward. The clearly defined projects on your list are more important right now.

Take Action

Use the five reasons listed above to remove unworthy projects from the master project list you created in Step 1: The Big Brain Dump. If you're honest with yourself, this exercise should eliminate at least half of your original list. Remember, you can add those projects back later if circumstances change, but right now you need to remain focused on the most worthwhile projects.

CHAPTER FIVE

Finding Your Most Important Project

STEP 3. PRIORITIZE THE REST

It's time to prioritize those projects that are still alive and well on your list. When prioritizing your projects, you have to decide what is most important to you.

For DIY home projects, I prefer to evaluate my list based on a project's impact on my quality of life versus the level of effort required to complete the project. I find the things that greatly improve quality of life at home are increased living space, added functionality, things working properly, organization, and efficiencies. Still important, but lower on the quality of life scale, are how a space makes me feel, if it is well furnished, if there is enough seating for company, if the space is well lit, and if it is kid-friendly. Other factors that are important when decorating but don't have a direct or measurable impact on quality of life are the colors in a space and aesthetic touches like wall decor and fabrics.

For level of effort, I consider if a project will be difficult to complete (high effort) or easy to complete (low effort), where effort is a combination of cost, time, and skill. What you consider high effort and what I consider high effort probably aren't the same. Level of effort must be based on what you think is a reasonable cost for a particular project, the time required to complete it, and whether or not you have the skills to do the work.

Measuring projects against quality of life and level of effort gives you a good framework to follow. I call it the Project Prioritization Matrix. To determine the importance of your projects, plot each project on the matrix according to how it aligns with the attributes on the x-axis and y-axis.

HOW TO READ THE MATRIX

There are four quadrants on the Project Prioritization Matrix. The vertical y-axis is for Quality of Life, and the horizontal x-axis represents Level of Effort. Notice the worst projects that offer no quality of life improvement and require a high level of effort are at the origin. This means the most desirable projects land in the upper right quadrant, which are relatively easy to complete and will greatly improve the quality of life in your home.

The label in each quadrant suggests the priority of the projects in that quadrant:

- **Must Do:** Projects in the upper right quadrant will improve your quality of life and are easy to do. These are your top priorities.
- **Maybe Do:** Projects in the upper left quadrant will improve your quality of life, but are harder to do. These are worth considering if the benefit far outweighs the effort required.
- **Might Do:** Projects in the bottom right quadrant are easy to do, but may have no impact on your quality of life. These are a low priority.
- **Don't Do:** Projects in the bottom left quadrant require the most effort and won't noticeably change the quality of life in your home. You shouldn't do these projects.

HOW TO USE THE MATRIX

To use the matrix, number your project list and then plot each project number on the matrix based on quality of life from no improvement to greatly improved and level of effort from easy to difficult.

If your project list is quite extensive, or you just want to make this exercise more fun, create a giant prioritization matrix. On a white board, chalkboard, or large blank wall create four quadrants with painter's tape. Write the name of each project on a sticky note, then plot them on the matrix. This is a fun way to get a spouse or friend involved too.

I want to share with you a few real-life project ideas and demonstrate how I plotted them on the matrix:

Project 1. Paint a focal wall in the bedroom.

I wanted to change the color of the wall behind our head-board, but a small color change wasn't going to have a considerable impact on my quality of life. On the plus side, painting a single wall is easy and quick, so the level of effort is low. That puts this project idea in the Might Do category.

Since it was easy and we had the paint on hand, we did this project. We love the new color and fresh feeling in our bedroom.

Project 2. Create a playroom under the stairs.

When we finished our basement we were left with a space under the stairs with an angled ceiling in the front and half-height space in the back. We've had under-the-stairs storage closets before and found them to be awkward spaces that were difficult to utilize well. We have a lot of other storage in this house, so the last thing we needed was another closet. Instead, we had the idea to turn the space into a playhouse for the kids. It would increase their living space and be a fun hideout, which I consider a great quality of life improvement.

We had most of the supplies—paint, carpet, kid-sized furniture—on hand, but some of it required DIY work which would take time. The level of effort was moderate. That put this project idea borderline between the Maybe Do and Must Do category.

Because our kids are cute, we gave in and made this a Must Do. We carpeted the space and moved their play kitchen and a small table in. We added a curtain in the door-way. The kids love their little hideout. We stopped short of truly "finishing" the space because we didn't need to do anything more to it for the boys to love it.

Project 3. Fix or replace the garage door opener.

Apparently the garage door opener installed when our house was built was not strong enough for a two-car garage door. It lasted less than four years. When it finally broke we were faced with a big bill for a new garage door opener and installation. With a harsh Minnesota winter fast approaching, we really wanted to park the cars inside. A new garage door opener would have been a huge quality of life improvement.

Unfortunately we have no experience repairing garage door openers, so the level of effort for us to fix it or install a new one ourselves would have been high. Initially that put this project into the Maybe Do category, but boy do I hate scraping snow and ice off of my car.

We almost held off on this project, even though winter was nearing. Then, we saw a Groupon deal for a local repair place, which made the level of effort easy and the price more affordable. So, we shifted this project from the Maybe Do to the Must Do quadrant and called in a professional to help. It was worth the expense, because the garage door opener was beyond repair and needed to be replaced.

Project 4. Paint the kitchen cabinets white.

I daydream of a white kitchen. Our current home is my first house without white cabinets. But cabinetry color is not going to noticeably improve our kitchen or our lives. We already have nice cabinets, but they just aren't white.

I've painted kitchen cabinets before and recall how time-consuming it is to tackle such a project. To hire out the work would be expensive. When I painted the cabinets in our first house it totally disrupted our use of the kitchen. I'm also a recovering perfectionist and, as hard as I try, I know I wouldn't get the quality of finish I want. The level of effort required for painting cabinets is pretty high in my book. Without a significant positive impact on quality of life and considering the difficulty level, this project landed in the Don't Do quadrant.

That's why I don't have a white kitchen now, because the level of effort required might not be worth the low impact on quality of life. Just because I like white cabinets does not make it a worthy project.

Online Video Bonus
Watch me use the Project Prioritization Matrix:
www.TealandLime.com/ProjectHomeBonus

Online Bonus
Download the *Project Home* Prioritization Matrix:
www.TealandLime.com/ProjectHomeBonus

TAKE ACTION

Use the steps above to plot your projects on the matrix. This is a great exercise to do with the other people that live in your home or help you with projects. It may stir up some discussion and lead to redefinition of projects or even removing projects from the list because they're not worth pursuing. This will help everyone get on the same page about which projects are most important.

You'll see how forcing yourself to use a priority matrix takes the emotion out of choosing and prioritizing projects. It allows you to evaluate them objectively, and more easily compare them to one another. The only thing left is deciding which project comes first in each priority group.

STEP 4. RANK THE BEST

In the last step of prioritization, you need to rank the projects in the order you plan to complete them. You can certainly rank all of the projects across the different quadrants, but I recommend focusing on the Must Do projects first. Then, you can move on to ranking the Might Dos and Maybe Dos.

Ranking can be as objective or subjective as you like. Personally, I like to choose an objective quality for ranking based on what is most important to me, and it can vary between the different quadrants of the prioritization matrix.

For example, in the Must Dos, where I know the project is easy and will greatly improve my quality of life, I don't care as much about small differences in time or money required to complete the projects. I know all of these projects will be worth the time and money. Instead, I care most about the impact on my quality of life. Therefore, I rank the Must Do projects based on quality of life. The #1 project will have the greatest impact on quality of life.

For the Maybe Dos, which are harder to do, but promise a quality of life improvement, I rank based on value. I want the biggest bang for my buck here. Projects that require the least effort (time and cost) and promise the biggest quality of life improvement—that is, the projects higher up and further to the right within that quadrant—rank higher.

For the Might Dos, you could delete these. They won't have a noticeable impact on your quality of life. But since they are easy, you may want to keep them on your list. These are good projects to do when you just want a quick, creative project. I rank these by time and cost. The quicker and cheaper, the better.

Lastly, the Don't Dos. Pretty self-explanatory, right? Remove these from your list. They're not even worth your effort to rank, because they are difficult and provide no benefit.

Take Action

Rank your project ideas. Simply transfer projects from your master list to the Ranked Priorities worksheet. Put them in the appropriate priority group (corresponding with the quadrants on the matrix—Must Do, Maybe Do, Might Do) and list them in rank order from most to least important.

Online Bonus
Download the *Project Home* Ranked Priorities worksheet at: www.TealandLime.com/ProjectHomeBonus

Your Clean Project List

When you're done with all four steps, you'll have your final project list in rank order. You might be tempted to think you just start at the top and go down the list. If money and time were no object, then you would be correct. But since we all have time and money constraints, the ranked project list simply becomes a tool for choosing your highest priorities, which are the projects to focus on first. You can jump around the list as needed to work within your budget and timeline. Just be careful not to let time and money spent on lower priority projects rob from the higher priority projects.

If you followed the four steps in this chapter and the last, you'll have a master project list that won't make you feel hopeless, frustrated, or tearful when you look at it. You know everything on this list is organized in order of importance, and the projects toward the top will greatly improve the quality of life in your home. You can repeat this four-step system to clean up your list anytime feels overwhelming.

Keep your list clean and organized. Once you have a prioritized project list to work from, don't add any new projects. Track new ideas on a separate list and include them in your next planning and prioritization session. At that point you can determine if they should jump the line ahead of other projects.

Knowing which project to start with is important, but it doesn't guarantee success. When you feel unmotivated, get stuck, or aren't sure what to do next *during* your project, it's handy to have a plan to refer to. Like I said at the beginning of this book, there isn't an instruction manual for creating a home. But you can write your own on a project-by-project basis.

PART TWO
Follow Through

Now that you have a list of prioritized and ranked projects, it's time to talk about getting those projects done. When was the last time you were successful at anything without a plan? You probably made dinner last night following a recipe, you figured out where your son's baseball game is by following a map, and you survived college with the help of a course syllabus and a counselor. All of those are plans. They help you follow a process or get from Point A to Point B.

I know right now making a plan for every home project sounds like extra work. However, the work you do to complete the steps in the second half of this book is key to the success of your project. And after you do project planning a few times it will get faster and easier. Try it out on one project and I am certain you'll continue to create these tools for every project afterward.

At the end of the last chapter you discovered your most important project—the one you should tackle next because it will have the biggest quality of life improvement for the least amount of effort. I want that project to be your muse for the rest of this book. Throughout the rest of the book you'll see

"TAKE ACTION" sections at the end of each chapter. If you take action while reading this part, by the end you'll have a complete project plan for your most important project.

Using the three main tools—scope, schedule, and budget —detailed in this part of the book may also further your project motivation and focus. Especially if you're a procrastinator or a worrier, these planning tools can help you feel more in control of the outcome of your project. With proper planning you'll be more likely to want to start working on your project right away.

THREE PARTS OF PROJECT QUALITY

A simple triangle will help you understand everything you need to know about good project management. The triangle is a way of understanding and controlling the quality of your project. Each side of the triangle represents one of the critical factors that determine quality. We'll talk about what each of these mean and how you work with them to get the best possible end result for any project on your to-do list.

This is the theory of triple constraints. It's a model for maintaining balance and making trade-offs between the three elements that define a project: scope, time, and cost.

Time and cost are obvious constraints because you're always limited on how much time and money you have available for a project. Time is how long a project takes from start to finish. Cost is the total cost to complete the project.

You may not be familiar with scope, though. In a project, scope is the list of things you want to do. Say you're making over a room and want to install new carpet, put up decorative wallpaper, replace the sofa, and hang new art. Those four tasks are the scope of your project.

The triangle is a reminder that the triple constraints must always be in balance. You cannot change one of the constraints without affecting at least one of the other two, or the quality of the entire project. If one of the constraints changes, one or both of the other two constraints must also change to bring the project back into balance.

You can't control all three constraints. That's to say, you can't expect to redecorate an entire room, get everything you want for less than $500, and do it in one afternoon. You must make trade-offs. You start by determining what is most important: Is it getting everything you want, spending less than $500, or finishing this afternoon? Whichever is the most important is your *fixed* constraint and the other two need to *flex* to meet it.

This model helps you follow through when life happens and things change, which they always do. Something costs more than expected (cost), a task takes longer than you thought (time), or you had a really great idea for something to add to your project (scope). When changes happen, you can revisit the triple constraints to see what you can do to get back on track.

CHAPTER SIX

Triple Constraints

Understanding how the triple constraints work is the key to organizing and completing a successful project. When one constraint changes, one or both of the other constraints must also change. If there is one constraint that cannot change—a fixed constraint—then the other two must remain flexible.

When I worked as a project manager, my main goal during early project meetings was to figure out the fixed constraint. The project sponsor always had one thing—scope, time, or cost—they cared about more than anything else, even though they weren't always forthcoming about it. Figuring out early on which constraint was fixed helped me successfully manage the project. If there were changes that might impact that constraint, I knew I needed to adjust one of the other constraints to stay on track. Often, I presented the other two constraints as options to the project sponsor when a project was in jeopardy. It went something like this: "If you don't want it to cost more, then do you want it to take longer or do you want to do less?" Assuming they wanted good quality, a time increase or scope reduction are the only two options given the cost constraint.

It's the same for you with your home projects. You can't control all three. Pick the one that is most important to you, then know that the other two may need to flex to keep the most important constraint in check. If you find you need to make an adjustment, you can choose which other constraint to change.

THE TRADE-OFFS

You will make trade-offs during your project. Every project has them. How you deal with them will determine the success of your project. Throughout your project, make sure the constraint you care about most stays under control.

If you find out halfway through your project that it's going to cost more than you planned, then you will need to reduce the scope, or take more time to complete the project in order to stay under budget. For example, if you forgot to plan for installation costs with your new carpet, meaning the actual cost is higher than planned, then you might need to skip the decorative wallpaper. By reducing scope (not installing wallpaper), and in turn some cost, you make up for the additional expense required to have the carpet installed.

If you run into time delays, you will need to either cut scope or increase the budget to complete the project on or ahead of time. For example, if you planned to install kitchen cabinets yourself to save money, but it took twice as long as you planned, then you might choose to hire a professional to install the tile faster than you could by yourself. By increasing the budget to get help installing the tile faster, you make up for some of the extra time it took to install the cabinets.

If you increase your scope by taking on additional work, your project is almost always going to cost more or take longer to complete or both. For example, say you were only planning to get new bedding for a quick bedroom makeover, but then you saw a headboard that would look amazing in the room. Adding a new headboard to the project is definitely going to cost more than the bedding alone and if you have to wait for the headboard to be delivered, it will take longer to finish the room. Major scope increases are usually the most detrimental type of change to a project, because they can only be accommodated with more time or money or both.

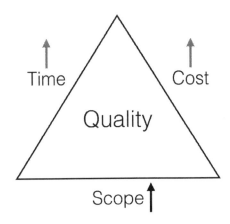

Beware of Scope Creep

Have you ever started on a project that you thought would only take a weekend? But by the end of the weekend you realized you were in way over your head? Did it seem like everything snowballed and got out of control?

Everyone focuses on time and money because they're straightforward to measure and track, but scope is the one to watch out for. Scope is what throws a project off. The project may appear to cost more or take longer, but often the cause can be traced back to an increase in scope. That's called scope creep.

Skip the Buffet

Most people approach home decorating like a buffet. It's all you can eat but you only get one plate. So, you pile that plate as high as you can with everything you can and make sure to plop a yummy dessert right on top. But if you've ever really juggled a full plate in a buffet line, then you know that as you keep adding more stuff on top, the risk of things falling off the plate increases. The same thing might be happening with your home projects.

I want you to think of your home projects more like packing a lunch box, specifically, a bento box with a lid. When you pack a bento box, you plan out your lunch to fill the compartments of the box. You can't pile it too high or the lid won't close. If you want to fit in that chocolate cake, you have to make room by removing something else. In the bento box analogy, if you want to add something to your project, you have to choose to remove something else.

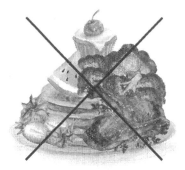 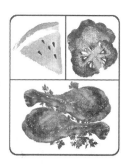

That is how you should view your home projects. You have limitations. If you want to stay under budget or keep on schedule, you have to choose what's in and what's out of scope.

TAKEAWAYS

- The theory of triple constraints is a model to help you understand the necessary trade-offs between scope, time, and cost for a successful project.
- Although most people focus on how much it costs and how long it takes, scope is the constraint to really

watch out for. A carefully managed scope can keep the budget and schedule in check.

Understanding the triple constraints—scope, cost, and time—is a good big picture overview of project management, but to put theory into practice we need to move in a lot closer. In the next chapter, we'll start with how to write a good scope definition for any project, how to get buy-in on your project ideas from your friends and family, how to define your project requirements, and how to manage scope throughout your project.

CHAPTER SEVEN

How to Define Your Project

The all you can eat buffet—a temptation to keep adding things to your project—ends with scope management. In this chapter, I want to set you up with the basics for project success. You'll learn how to:

- Craft a crystal clear scope definition so there's no question about what your project includes.
- Plan for the four key resources every project needs.
- Get buy-in from everyone involved to avoid disagreements later on.

HOW TO CRAFT YOUR SCOPE DEFINITION

Every great project starts with a clear scope definition, which makes it easier to watch out for scope creep throughout the project. One of the biggest reasons any project gets off track is scope creep—when the project grows little by little and the increased time and money required to complete all the changes sneak up on you.

Did I just describe every home project you've ever done?

To avoid scope creep, you must clearly identify the scope of the project upfront with a scope definition. A well-defined scope tells you two very important things:

1. What's in scope.
2. What's out of scope.

During the project, you have to stick to your defined scope. If you deviate and start adding things to the project, it will almost always cost more money or take more time to complete the project. It's the reason most "weekend projects" last for weeks or months. A good scope definition can prevent those longer-than-intended projects.

The goal is to be clear and concise. "Redecorate the bedroom" is a bad scope definition. It's too vague. It needs more detail.

What's in Scope?

To better define your scope, start with what's "in scope." Your scope definition should clearly and specifically state what is in scope. The more detailed you can make your scope definition the better.

Consider these questions to get started:

- What room are you working on?
- Are you replacing furniture, painting, or buying new things?
- What will you do yourself and what will you hire out?

Example: *Our master bedroom makeover includes painting the walls, rearranging the furniture, and hanging new artwork (already purchased). We'll do all the work ourselves.*

What's out of Scope?

Next, you need to define what's "out of scope." A great scope definition is crystal clear. That clarity comes from clearly and specifically stating what is out of scope. Knowing what is *not* included in your project is *as important as knowing what is.*

Consider these questions to get started:

- Are there nearby rooms or part of this room that are not included in the project?
- What things in the room will NOT be changed or replaced?
- What tasks will be saved for another project later or included in a different project?

Example: *For this project we will keep existing furniture and flooring. This makeover does not include making any additional purchases.*

Together, the two parts of your scope definition form a clear description of what is and what is not included in the project. By being clear about what the project does and does not include upfront, you increase the chances the project will be successful.

Example: *Our weekend master bedroom makeover will include painting the walls, rearranging the furniture, and hanging new artwork (already purchased). We'll do all the work ourselves. For this project we will keep existing furniture and flooring. This makeover does not include making any new purchases.*

In the example project, the scope helps clearly identify what a "master bedroom makeover" entails. It becomes clear that this is not a complete bedroom redo, nor is it necessarily the last makeover for the room. It provides a clear definition of what will make this project successful.

If you're working with someone, like your spouse, on the

project, then a clear scope definition can help you get on the same page about what's included and what's not.

Online Bonus
Download the *Project Home* Scope Definition worksheet at:
www.TealandLime.com/ProjectHomeBonus

KEY RESOURCES EVERY PROJECT NEEDS

Every project needs resources—the people, time, money, and tools/supplies available to complete the project. When determining your scope, you should identify your resources early on—what do you have at your disposal for the project in these four areas:

1. **People** - Who will be working on the project? What skills do they have? When are they available to work on the project?

2. **Time** - When do you need the project to be done? How much time does each person have each day to work on the project? Is there a project deadline? (For example, the bedroom project must be completed before overnight guests arrive.)

3. **Money** - How much money do you have for the project? What ways could you save money on this project? Are you willing to put in the extra effort or time to save money?

4. **Tools/Supplies** - What do you already have that you can use for the project? For DIY projects, which tools and supplies do you already have on hand? For all decorating projects, you should shop your home first. Decor from other rooms may work for your makeover. To find out how to maximize what you

already have, check out my book *Free Decorating.*

When considering your resources, it's important to identify both what you have and what you don't have. Make a plan to get the resources you're missing. We'll talk more specifically about people resources in Chapter Ten and money resources in Chapters Eleven and Twelve.

GETTING BUY-IN

I hope you have people to help you with your projects. Help is wonderful, and people are one of the most valuable resources on any project. But sometimes people cause new problems. What if you're not on the same page? Misunderstandings, miscommunication, and disagreements can derail a project faster than anything else.

If you're working with a spouse, friend, or other family member on your project, you need to get buy-in first. Buy-in is agreement on what the project includes, the scope of the project, and how it will be managed. This is also a critical step for making sure everyone on the project feels valued and knows that their input is important.

A project charter is the best way to get buy-in from your helpers. A "charter" sounds formal, but it's actually a simple document that wields a lot of power. While it may sound like a stuffy corporate project artifact, the concept behind a project charter can be helpful at home. In business and at home, a project charter is used to ensure alignment and get buy-in and approval of the project. Project charters can vary from simple to complex.

For home projects, these are the key elements of a project charter:

- **Problem Statement** - What problem are you trying to solve with this project? Another way to think about this is to ask this question: What quality of life improvement are you trying to make?

- **Scope Definition** - What is in scope and out of scope?
- **Success Criteria** - What do you hope to gain from this project?
- **Project Team** - Who is sponsoring, or paying for, the project, who is managing the project, and who is doing the work? For home projects you might play all of these roles yourself. If you plan to have anyone else help, identify them here.
- **Critical Project Resources** - Of the four types of resources listed in the previous section, are there any special resources required for project success? This could be a certain person you need available to help or a special tool you need. Not having this resource would seriously cripple the project.
- **Approvals** - At least the sponsor and project manager should sign off on the project charter. In a business environment, the sponsor's signature indicates approval to start the project. The project manager's signature is a commitment to deliver the project as described. At home you, and those helping you with the project, are making similar commitments.

A simple one-page document covering these key elements and signed by everyone involved signifies alignment on what is included in the project and serves as an agreement to go forward with the project.

Online Bonus

Download the *Project Home* Project Charter worksheet at:
www.TealandLime.com/ProjectHomeBonus

For a home project, a project charter, or at least the idea of alignment, can be helpful if anyone else is involved in the project. Maybe your spouse wants some input, but doesn't want an active role in the project. Maybe your parents are loaning you money for a renovation. It's nice to keep them in the loop too. A basic project charter can help you get these "sponsors" in your life on the same page and avoid controversy later. Your husband won't be able to claim he had no idea you were planning to gut the bathroom. Your parents will be more receptive to pleas for additional funding later in the project if you gave them the courtesy of buy-in to a good plan early on.

TAKE ACTION

- Download the *Project Home* Scope Definition worksheet and write the scope definition for your most important project. Clearly detail what is included and what is not.
- Download the *Project Home* Project Charter worksheet to document alignment on the problem statement, scope definition, success criteria, project team, and critical resources for your project.

Hooray! You've taken step one toward a more successful project. Altogether, your scope definition, success criteria (covered in Chapter Three), and project charter, which captures all of the above, set the stage for project success. These are the earliest planning tasks in any project and also some

of the most important. How you define your scope and success criteria will shape your project. In the next chapter, we'll
go one step further and create project requirements so
there's no confusion about what needs to get done.

CHAPTER EIGHT

What Are Your Requirements?

The next step after getting alignment on your project charter is determining your detailed requirements—exactly what your finished project needs to meet to be successful. In this chapter you'll learn how to:

- Write project requirements that detail exactly what needs to be done.
- Manage changes to your project so you can stay on schedule and on budget.

CREATING CLEAR AND SPECIFIC REQUIREMENTS

Good requirements are specific and measurable. A requirement defines a need. There are two broad types of requirements: must-have and nice-to-have. Must-have requirements must be met for the project to be a success. Nice-to-have requirements could be cut if needed to keep the project on schedule or under budget. For example, a must-have requirement is the bathroom will have a vanity, and a nice-to-have requirement is the vanity will have a marble top. The vanity is critical to the success of a bathroom remodel, but whether it's marble or another material is less important. It's a really good idea to identify if a requirement is a must-have or a nice-to-have upfront, so you know how to manage it later on. Addressing an issue with meeting a must-have requirement would be a priority over finishing a nice-to-have requirement.

Here are a couple simple examples of requirements:

- The walls will be painted with one coat of primer, followed by two coats of paint.
- The paint will be a water-based satin finish.

Notice the requirement does not say what color paint? That is a design choice. Notice the requirement does not say how the paint should be applied, brush or roller? That is an implementation choice. Requirements are usually functional and do not specify design or implementation.

Listing requirements that state what should *not* be done might seem helpful, but they can cause confusion. It is best to frame requirements in the positive. Here's how to rephrase a negative requirement:

Negative: The wood trim will not be painted.

Positive: The wood trim will remain as is with the current stain color.

Both say not to paint the trim, but the first one is less clear. It says not to paint the trim, but it doesn't say not to stain it. By rephrasing the requirement to a positive and adding more detail, it is clear the wood trim should stay in its current condition.

Being able to state your project requirements clearly is

not only helpful when hiring a contractor to do work for you, but it's also helpful if you are tackling a project on your own or with the help of friends and family. Clearly stated requirements eliminate confusion.

For small projects, you may not need to list out detailed requirements like the examples above. That might take longer than the project itself! Less formality is okay for small projects. For example, you might just write one simple requirement, like, "I'm going to prime and paint the walls in the office."

For larger projects, like a remodel, requirements are critical. Requirements should be agreed upon and understood by all parties involved (from your spouse to helpful family or friends to hired professionals). When we started our basement remodel, we had several meetings with our contractor about requirements before signing the contract, which included a list of the detailed requirements we agreed upon.

One major, nonnegotiable requirement for a home is that it meets building codes. You can trust your contractor or builder to ensure code compliance because it will be required for their work to pass inspections. But the minimum required by code may not be what you want. For example, our building code specifies placement of electrical outlets. For the large 17-ft wall in our basement, only one outlet is required if it was placed in the center of the wall. The contractor assumed the minimum is what we would want and only planned for one outlet on that wall in his cost estimate. We plan to eventually center a freestanding ethanol fireplace on that wall. We did not want the only outlet to end up behind the fireplace. We required our contractor to put two outlets on that wall to meet code and avoid having an outlet in the center of the wall.

Kitchen remodeling and closet organization are other great examples of where clear and specific requirements are critical. If you have 25 dresses to hang and your new closet plan only has full-length hanging room for ten dresses, that's a problem. Likewise, kitchens have tons of requirements for storage, accommodating small appliances, and creating the ideal work triangle. Identifying upfront how much and what type of space is needed is critical.

Requirements are needs that must be planned for in the project and decisions that need to be made. Some decisions can wait until later in a project, like which color to paint, with little impact on the success of the project. Other decisions, like wanting to paint the walls in the first place, need to be made upfront to ensure project success. Any decisions on project details that will have an impact on time and cost must be made early on in the project because they are a critical input to time and cost estimates.

One other note about requirements—it can be difficult to get started. The formality of it or the finality of it feels scary. If you're stuck, just start writing things down—as the ideas start to flow you can go back and reshape them into good requirements later on. You'll want to finalize your requirements before starting the project, but don't worry about making them perfect on the first pass.

How to Handle Change

Once you have a clear, agreed upon scope definition and you've created detailed requirements, your job is to watch out for scope creep as you work through your project. Those seemingly simple little things you add to a project along the way add up over time and can cause you to miss your deadline or go over budget. You need to stay on top of changes, even small ones, to your project.

Change over the course of a project is inevitable. How you handle change is important. Change can come about voluntarily, when you want to add something to the project that was previously out of scope. Change can occur when something you thought during planning was wrong; for example, your estimate was wrong or a resource is unavailable. Changes may also come from sources completely out of your control, like an unexpected delay or issue.

Although you can't plan for every possible change or issue, the effect of scope changes should never be a surprise. As soon as a potential change is introduced, it should be analyzed.

When changes do arise, don't ignore them. Learn about them.

- What caused the change?
- What impact does the change have (money, time, scope, people, quality)?
- What can you do to eliminate or minimize the change?

In the best-case scenario, your project can absorb a change (meaning it won't have a big impact on time or money) or you have enough contingency to cover the change (we'll discuss that in Chapter Twelve). In the worst-case scenario, you'll have to remove something from the project (de-scope) to make up for the loss caused by the change. For every change, you need to ask, "Does this change the scope of my project?"

If you planned to paint your room blue but then decided to use some gray paint you had in the garage, there is no impact on the project timeline or cost. As long as you have enough leftover gray paint to complete your project, you can include that change without worry—it's not a scope change.

If you planned to leave the ceiling white, but over the course of painting the walls gray decided you would like to paint the ceiling gray to match, then you need to more closely examine the impact of that change. Painting the ceiling will take additional time. Painting the ceiling might cost more, if you need to buy additional paint or get drop cloths to cover the furniture below. This seemingly simple change is exactly what scope creep is about. It won't seem like a big deal, until you realize you don't have enough paint and you have to run to the paint store late at night to buy more. Suddenly, in addition to the time to paint the ceiling, you have to add in transit time to and from the paint store, idle time waiting for the paint color to be mixed, and the additional cost of more paint. The magnitude of the scope change starts to snowball and impacts the other two project constraints: time and cost.

If a change impacts the scope of your project, then the next question is: What does that mean? More money, more time, or both?

If you decide to go forward with a change that impacts the time or cost of your project, you'll have to change your schedule or budget. If you properly manage time and cost with the tools I'll share in the next two chapters, then the potential impact of a scope change is easier to spot and stop.

The key thing to remember is that scope can be managed. It may not be as easy to track as time and cost, but if you pay attention to it, it's easier to manage. If you don't want the project to take longer or cost more, then actively avoid scope changes, meaning anything that adds time or cost to the project. It's as simple as that.

TAKE ACTION

- Write a first draft of your detailed requirements—the needs that will be met—for your most important project.
- Now make a second pass through your requirements list to fill in any gaps. Throughout this process refer back to your scope definition (don't add any requirements for things that are out of scope!) and your success criteria (make sure all your requirements contribute to project success).
- Monitoring for scope creep and managing change in your project starts now! Keep a close eye on any changes that may impact the scope, time, or cost of your project. If changes arise, analyze them quickly to determine the impact. In upcoming chapters I'll share a couple options for mitigating changes.

You're doing a great job! You've completed your scope definition, gotten buy-in on your project charter, and drafted your project requirements. Now I bet you're eager to book some time on your calendar to get your project done. But before you can schedule your project, you have to figure out how long your project, and the tasks to complete it, will take. I'll show you how in the next chapter.

CHAPTER NINE

Time Estimating

Time management revolves around a schedule. But before you can make a schedule and figure out when your project will be done, you need to do a few other steps. In this section, I'll show you how to:

- Create a work breakdown of all the tasks in your project so nothing slips through the cracks.
- Estimate the time each task will take so you can determine the total time required for your project.

You'll learn how to use these two inputs to create your project schedule in the next chapter.

WORK BREAKDOWN

First, you need to create a work breakdown. This is a complete list of all the known tasks in the project—no more, no less. This step helps you identify often overlooked tasks and breaks down the whole project into smaller chunks that are easier to estimate.

I want to share with you my favorite interactive way to create a work breakdown. This is the best way to do it whether you are by yourself or working in a group. I highly recommend doing this exercise with anyone who will help you with the project—your spouse, kids, or other family and friends.

You'll need a blank wall, sticky notes, and markers. Start by writing the name of your project on a sticky note, then put it on the wall. Your goal with this exercise is to identify each task in your project. Brainstorm tasks, one per sticky note, and stick them on the wall. Refer to your project requirements to trigger tasks. What tasks must be completed to meet each requirement?

It's best to start each task note with a verb. What is the action that needs to be done? Paint, hang, move, clean, etc. So, instead of writing "curtains," you would write, "hang curtains" or "iron curtains" or "sew curtains." The verb adds clarity to what actually needs to be done.

Once you have ten to fifteen tasks, start organizing them into groups of related tasks. These groups become the phases of your project. For example, a dresser refinishing project includes a preparation phase, a painting phase, and a cleanup phase. Larger projects may have more phases.

As they become apparent, write the name of each phase on a sticky note. Put the project phases in a row below the project name. Then, arrange the tasks for each phase below the phase name. Continue adding tasks to each phase until you're confident you've included all the tasks required for each phase.

Project	Dresser Makeover		
Phases	Preparation	Painting	Cleanup
Tasks	Sand Dresser	Prime the Dresser	Put Drawers Back In / Wash Paint Brush
	Remove Drawers	Paint First Coat	

Review your individual tasks to see if you can break them down any further. It's a good idea to decide on a standard task "size." In large software development projects that spanned months or years, we broke down tasks until they were eighty hours of work (two weeks) or less. For a home project, you need to decide on a manageable task size and break down all parts of your project to that size. For large home projects or renovations that might be three to five days, for small projects like this example it might be tasks that can be completed in less than two hours. The idea is to make sure you are getting to a consistent level of specificity for your tasks. For example, a task like "paint the dresser" could take several days and is rather vague. To make estimating and completing that broad task easier, it can be split into three new tasks: prime the dresser, paint the first coat, paint the second coat. The more granular your tasks, the more accurately you can estimate how long they will take to complete.

Once you're done, keep your sticky notes on the wall because you'll need them again in the next step.

Online Video Bonus
Watch me create a work breakdown for a project:
www.TealandLime.com/ProjectHomeBonus

TIME ESTIMATES

I know estimating may sound boring or complicated, but it's a critical step for making a realistic project schedule. A little time spent planning upfront can save you time and money in the long run. I promise I'll keep it simple.

A time estimate is how long you think each task will take to complete. Think back to the last three small projects you did around the house. Did they take less time or more time than you thought? I'm guessing they took more time. Projects usually take longer than we think they will. People in general tend to be optimistic. For that reason, we're usually bad at estimating the total time a project will take. And the bigger the project, the worse the estimate gets. So instead, it's best to estimate smaller chunks and add them all up. You want to estimate at the *task* level, and the work breakdown you just created is perfect for this. By estimating each individual task and adding them all up, you'll create a more accurate project time estimate.

There are two types of time estimates: effort and duration. Effort is the exact amount of work time a task takes to complete. Duration is the total elapsed time to complete the task. A task may take only twenty minutes (effort), but if you can only work on it five minutes a day, then it will take four days (duration) to complete. You really can't figure out duration for most tasks until you build your schedule, so focus on effort-based time estimates. How much active time will it take you to complete a task?

For some tasks, you should also consider lag time. Lag time is the wait time at the end of the task before you can start the next task, for example, waiting for paint to dry before painting the next coat or waiting for a piece of furniture to be delivered before you can place it in the room. Lag time should be included in your time estimate because it directly impacts when you can start the next step in the project. Add your effort-based estimate for painting to the lag time for drying to get a total time for that task. Lag times like the delivery example will be important for project scheduling but don't need to be added to your time estimates at this point. We'll talk more about lag times and how to use them to your advantage later in the next chapter.

Back to the sticky notes. Now, you'll need a different colored marker. Revisit each task on your sticky notes. Estimate the amount of time to complete the task. Add lag times where appropriate. Write the time estimate in red marker on the corner of the sticky note. Then, add together the time estimates for all the tasks in each phase. Write the total for each phase on the sticky note at the top of each phase column. Then add up the totals for each of the phases to get a total time estimate for the entire project.

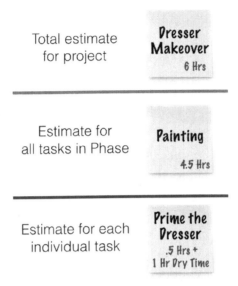

Total estimate for project	**Dresser Makeover** 6 Hrs
Estimate for all tasks in Phase	**Painting** 4.5 Hrs
Estimate for each individual task	**Prime the Dresser** .5 Hrs + 1 Hr Dry Time

You just estimated how much time you need to complete your project. But, at this point, you still don't know when your project will be done. Just because your total estimate is eight hours, doesn't mean you only need one day for the project. Only your project schedule can tell you that.

Online Video Bonus

Watch me create time estimates for a project:
www.TealandLime.com/ProjectHomeBonus

Now, you might be wondering how to actually estimate a task. If you've done the task before, you'll have some idea of how long it will take. But if it's something you've never done before, how do you estimate the time? Read on for several easy methods.

More Accurate Estimates

Are you overly optimistic? Do you always think something will take less time than it really does? I think that's a natural human tendency, but when it comes to project planning it can get us into big trouble. A little math and history can help us do better.

Here are five ways to more accurately estimate the time required to complete a task:

1. **Historical - Compare to Past** - If you've done the *same task* in the past and know how long it actually took, include at least that much time in your estimate. For example, if you want to paint your dining room and you know it took three hours to paint a similar-sized bedroom, you should estimate at least three hours to paint the dining room. If you do a lot of home projects, it's a wise idea to keep a log of the actual time it takes to complete tasks to use for future planning. Past performance is the best indicator of future performance.

2. Analogous - Compare to Similar Task - If you've done a *very similar task* in the past and know how long it actually took, you can use that as a basis for estimating this new task. Adjust for any differences in the new task. For example, if you need to estimate how long it will take to plant a shrub, you could use your past experience planting a tree as a reference point. You know it took one hour to dig a hole and transplant the tree. You know the hole for the shrub won't need to be as large, so you estimate slightly less time to dig a hole and transplant the shrub.

3. **Expert Judgment - Expert Opinion or Research** - If you have not done a similar task before,

find out if someone else has. Ask knowledgeable friends and family or search online for how long the task might take. Use your research to make an informed time estimate.

4. **Parametric** - A parametric estimate is when you determine the time it takes to finish one thing and multiply it by the total number of things to be completed. When I decided on a whim to rip the carpet off the stairs to reveal the wood treads in our first home, it took me about half an hour to pull the carpet staples from one step. I multiplied that by the remaining steps, and I knew I had five to six more hours of pulling staples in my future. This type of estimate works well with known entities and things that are very similar. It is not as effective for tasks that are different, like installing hardwood versus installing tile. You could use parametric estimating to determine how long it will take to install hardwood in five different rooms, but you should estimate installing tile in the last room separately. The task is too different to assume the same time estimate would apply.

5. **PERT Estimate - Accounting for the Best- and Worst-Case Scenarios** - The Program Evaluation and Review Technique, or PERT, method was developed by the Navy in the 1950s and is one of the most widely used models for time estimating. Some organizations even mandate its use. This method is also sometimes called the "three-point estimate," because the calculation is a weighted average of three estimates. You need to estimate the most likely (ML) time it will take to complete the task, optimistic (O) time it will take to complete the task, and pessimistic

(P) time it will take to complete the task:

PERT Formula: (O + 4ML + P)/6

Using this formula helps balance out overly optimistic or pessimistic estimators, which is especially helpful when you have several people working on estimates.

At home, I like this method because it allows you to take into account a best-case and worst-case scenario. For example, you might optimistically (O) estimate it will take four hours to tile a backsplash, assuming you have help and all the tools and supplies on hand. For your most likely (ML) estimate, you think it will take five hours because you will probably have to run to the home improvement store once for something you forgot. Pessimistically (P), if you don't have anyone to help you, then you estimate it will take eight hours. If you plug all those numbers into the formula:

$$(O + 4M + P)/6 = (4 + 4(5) + 8)/6 = 5.33$$

The resulting estimate is 5.33 hours. Now you know you better set aside more than an afternoon to do your tiling project.

On a few small tasks time estimating may not seem that important. But when you have a long list of tasks in a project (just look at how many are involved in painting a dresser!), then every estimating error compounds until your entire projected timeline is completely off. The few moments you put into more accurate estimates now will save you minutes, hours, even days over the course of your project.

TAKE ACTION

- Break out the sticky notes and markers again! It's time to create your work breakdown. Capture all the tasks that need to be completed to meet all of your project requirements.
- After all of your tasks are up on the wall and arranged into project phases, go back through and estimate the time to complete each task. Total all of your estimates for each phase, then total each phase to get a project total.
- One minute now can save you hundreds later. I challenge you to review your estimates once more and try one of the five techniques for more accurate estimates. Pro tip: Use all five techniques where they make the most sense to improve your estimates.

You're almost there. The next step is the big one. Your work breakdown and time estimates are the two key inputs for your project schedule. Now you're ready to find out when your project will realistically be complete. In the next chapter, I'll show you how to use your task list from the work breakdown and your estimates to determine the best starting point for your project, the logical sequence of tasks, and when you can expect your project to be done if all goes well.

CHAPTER TEN

How to Create a Project Schedule

You're ready to build your project schedule, which will not only tell you when your project will be finished (Yay!), but also when each task in the project will be worked on. In this chapter you'll learn how to:

- Identify dependencies so you can understand how project tasks are related to each other.
- Sequence the tasks in your project in the most logical way (and usually the fastest way to get it done).
- Take advantage of lag and lead times to make the most of your project time.

We'll finish up with a simple way to make your project schedule and figure out when your project will be done if everything goes as planned.

WHAT TO DO FIRST, THEN NEXT

My son (currently in second grade) was so excited to tell me all about his math class yesterday. They're learning order of operations—a model for deciding whether to multiply, subtract, divide, or add first in complex equations. He was most excited to share the handy mnemonic for remembering the correct order: Purple Elephants May Destroy A School, which means Parenthesis, Exponents, Multiplication, Division, Addition, Subtraction. (I learned it as Please Excuse My Dear Aunt Sally, but I guess that's not silly enough to stick with kids these days.) I wish the order of operations for tasks in a project were as easy to figure out.

While there isn't a mnemonic for determining the right order to complete the tasks in your project, there are a few simple steps you can take. Deciding the order of events in a project is called sequencing. The purpose of sequencing is to complete your project in the most efficient way, without wasted time. Sequencing includes identifying relationships between tasks (dependencies), finding the best starting point for your project, putting tasks in a logical order, and understanding lag and lead times for each task that can help you make the most of your time.

Identifying Dependencies

The relationships between tasks in a project are called dependencies. Knowing task dependencies is critical for sequencing. Most dependencies are either finish-to-start, meaning one task must finish before the other task can start, or start-to-start, meaning one task must start before the other task can start but the first task does not have to be finished before the second task starts. In a finish-to-start dependency, a dresser must be primed and dry before you can start painting it. In a start-to-start dependency, you must start applying tile mastic before you can start placing tiles, but you don't have to apply all the mastic before placing tiles. For a start-to-start dependency, once both tasks are started, they can happen in parallel.

Most projects are filled with finish-to-start dependencies. Many times this is unavoidable, especially if you're doing the project by yourself. Most of the tasks will be finish-to-start, because you're the only one that can do the work. Another common constraint is tool availability. If you and your spouse each want to hang a piece of art but you only have one hammer to put the nail in the wall, then you have constraint which forces a finish-to-start dependency: hanging one piece, then the other.

Start-to-start dependencies are great to take advantage of in projects where you have more than one person. I love having my son help put together IKEA furniture. Because I have his help, while he is unpacking the pieces, I can start reading the directions and putting part of the furniture together. This case is a start-to-start dependency because as soon as the unpacking starts, the assembly can start (assuming I can "read" IKEA's wordless directions—sometimes I need my son's help with that). When you have help in a project, identifying these start-to-start dependencies helps you figure out where you can divide and conquer to get more done in the same amount of time.

For an easier to manage project, only focus on true dependencies. Don't add dependencies where they're not necessary. For example, don't make installing tile in the shower dependent on replacing the vanity top. They're unrelated. Adding unnecessary dependencies creates unnecessary constraints on your project. Every task in a project will not have a dependency—when you're decorating a living room, you can purchase a lamp any time. It's not dependent on any other task.

Identifying dependencies is important to help you decide where to start on a project and the best path to take through the tasks. Here are three ways to document your project dependencies:

1. Go back to your task sticky notes from the work breakdown exercise. Number each task. Then in an opposite corner of the sticky note, write the numbers for any tasks that particular task is dependent on. Hang in there; for projects with many tasks and dependencies, this can get overwhelming fast. This method is best for small projects with few tasks.

#3	#7	#5 3, 7
Remove Drawers	Remove Drawer Handles	Sand Dresser

2. For a more visual approach, move your sticky notes to a large piece of paper or poster board and draw arrows between tasks that are related. The arrowhead should point to the task that is dependent upon the other task to complete. The task at the tail end of the arrow needs to finish before the task at the arrowhead can start. If you're into conspiracy theories or have a corkboard, you could use pushpins and yarn to link related tasks. Try using a different color pushpin for the "arrowhead"—that is the task that is dependent on the other task.

3. For the stuffy corporate method, use a spreadsheet or table to keep track of dependencies. List out all the tasks from your work breakdown and number them. Create a dependency column to document the task number for any dependencies. For example, if Task #5 is dependent on Task #3 and Task #7, then add "3, 7" in the dependency column for Task #5. This means

Task #5 cannot start until Tasks #3 and 7 are finished.

Find Your Starting Point

The simple act of identifying dependencies makes it easier to find a starting point for your project. You want to look for the task that is the first logical thing to do for the project. One easy way to find a starting point is to identify which task most other tasks depend on. That's your lead domino that starts the chain reaction. In a room makeover project, you might have many tasks dependent on the walls being painted first. Therefore, painting the walls is a logical starting point. Your first task should be one that will clear the most dependencies down the line.

You can also work backwards to find the starting point for any chain of dependencies. For example, if you're installing new carpet, then adding the baseboard is the last step. If you follow the dependencies backwards from that task, you'll eventually come to laying the carpet pad as the first step in the chain of events that need to happen to install the carpet.

Putting Tasks in a Logical Order

Once you understand the work in your project, the dependencies, and the best starting point, then you're ready to sequence the tasks. The easiest way to determine the order of tasks is by using a simple network logic diagram. I know, another stuffy corporate term, but it's easier than it sounds. In a network logic diagram there's a box for each task and arrows between the tasks to show relationships. The diagram is organized into work streams of related tasks.

The work breakdown you created earlier lists all your tasks, but it does not prescribe the order in which to complete the tasks. The network logic diagram is a reordering of the work breakdown to show the logical order the tasks should be completed in.

To create a network logic diagram, start with your first task in a box (your project starting point) on the left side of your diagram. The last task in the project will be on the right side of the diagram. From there, put the tasks into logical order, keeping the task dependencies in mind. If one task cannot be complete until another task finishes, the second task should be shown to the right of the first task with an arrow connecting them. If a task is unrelated to the first task, start another work stream (row) on the diagram. Merge work streams where a dependency occurs.

I first learned how to create network logic diagrams with an example showing the tasks involved in making a simple cup of tea. Maybe my similar example of how I make a complicated, but yummy cup of morning coffee will help you:

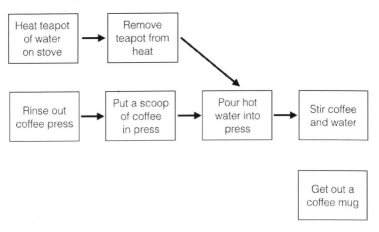

Obviously, a network logic diagram for a five-minute task like making a cup of coffee is overkill, but I think you can see how this type of diagram can help you plan a more complex project. Now, make yourself a cup of coffee and create a network logic diagram for your project.

To get started, try rearranging the sticky notes from your work breakdown into a network logic diagram. Draw or tape arrows between the sticky notes to show the relationships between the tasks.

The dependencies you identified earlier drive the logical order of the tasks. Also, notice how there are several tasks that can be completed in parallel with other tasks. In my coffee example, I get the coffee press ready while the water heats on the stove. Those are called parallel work streams— tasks that can occur at the same time because there are no dependencies between them. When there is a dependency between two or more tasks, the network logic diagram shows the logical order in which the tasks should be completed and where work streams converge or diverge.

The network logic diagram is not a schedule of activities. The network logic diagram simply helps you visualize the

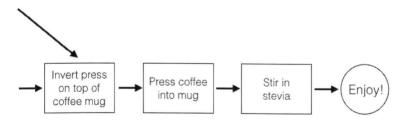

order of work and how many potential work streams you have for a project. When tasks appear in parallel on a network logic diagram, it does not mean you're going to do them at the same time; it simply means logically, if there were no other constraints, they could be done at the same time. The logical sequence of tasks with dependencies shows the order in which they must occur in relation to each other but not within the project as a whole. The actual order and timing of tasks are determined during scheduling.

Finding Hidden Time

Lag and lead times are your golden opportunities to use your project time more efficiently. As I mentioned in the estimating section, lag time is the time delay between when one task finishes and before the next task can start—how far a task must follow behind another task. Lead time is potential to get a head start on a task. Understanding lag and lead times can help you maximize your time on a project by finding hidden time opportunities in your schedule.

Lag times sound negative, but they can be used to your project's advantage. Although you have to plan for required lag times in the project schedule, lag time is also an opportunity to get something else done. Since you know your time estimates and dependencies, you can find another task to complete during a lag time. For example, if the drywall installer tapes and muds the drywall on Monday, he has to wait for it to dry fully before he can start sanding on Wednesday. The lag time between mudding and sanding is two days. During the lag time you could lay the floor tile to keep the project moving forward.

Lead time is an opportunity to get a head start on a task while another task is still being finished. For example, when painting, you're supposed to cut in the trim and then roll paint on the wall. When my husband and I paint a room, I cut in one wall to start, then while I cut in the other walls my husband starts rolling paint on the first wall. Instead of waiting for all the walls to be cut in, my husband uses the lead time while I finish cutting in the other walls to start rolling paint on the first wall.

You might initially think of lead time as the wait time for a special order item, like an upholstered sofa in a custom fabric. While that is one type of lead time, and you should see what other project tasks you can do while waiting for the sofa, the most advantageous lead times are found in tasks that have no dependencies, meaning they aren't dependent on anything to get started. Those are the tasks you have an opportunity to start or finish early. In my coffee example, I need to get out a coffee cup before I press the coffee, but I've got a few minutes of lead time. I can get out the coffee cup any time before the coffee is ready to go in it. It's not dependent on any other tasks, so I usually grab it after I rinse the coffee press, while I am still waiting for the water to finish heating. If I wait to get the coffee mug until all the other tasks are done and the coffee is ready to press, then I waste a little bit of time when the coffee is ready but the mug is not. Get your project done faster by finding lead opportunities to get a head start.

BUILDING YOUR PROJECT SCHEDULE

Okay, now you're ready to create your project schedule. This is your time-based plan for completing the project. Even though you know the time your project will take to complete and the logical order in which to do the tasks, you don't know when the project will be done until it's scheduled.

The schedule has four inputs:

1. Work breakdown (your tasks)
2. Time estimates (how long each task takes)
3. Dependencies (the order in which to do the tasks)
4. Resources (who will do the tasks)

You've already made the work breakdown and time estimates and you understand your dependencies. The last input is resources. Resources are the people doing the work. Who is going to work on the project—you, your spouse, a friend, your dad, a contractor?

For each person working on the project you need to know:

- How much time do they have to work on the project and when?
- When are they unavailable? (These are their non-working times or days.)
- What skills do they have? (This is important for knowing what tasks to assign them.)

The easiest way to create your project schedule is to use a calendar. I like the big desk or wall calendars from the office store. Start creating your schedule by writing a list of resources and the times they are available on each day. Cross off any non-working days when no resources are available. Non-working days are days when no project work will be done.

Once you have your resource availability filled in, you can slot in the tasks that need to be completed. Remember to put them in logical order based on your dependencies and your network logic diagram. Assign each task to the right person and make the task span enough working hours for completion. A single task might span several days depending on the resource's availability and how long you estimate the task will take. When using a monthly calendar, I like to use the larger task groupings or phases from the work breakdown to build out the schedule.

Jackie					
José		6	Jackie - 2 7	Jackie - 2 / José - 2 8	José - 2 9
Pad					

Install cabinets & counter

Assemble cabinets

| 11 | Jackie - 2 / José - 2 12 | 13 | Jackie - 2 / Pad - 2 14 | Jackie - 2 / Pad - 2 15 | Jackie - 2 16 |

Install tile

Install tile — Install sink & fridge

Finish baseboard & trim

| 18 | 19 | 20 | 21 | 22 | 23 |

In the online bonus, I've included a schedule planner with a monthly view and a two-day view, which is ideal for keeping a more detailed task-level plan. For more complex projects, I recommend using the two-day planner and detailing out the resources and time for each specific task.

Online Bonus
Download the *Project Home* Schedule Planner:
www.TealandLime.com/ProjectHomeBonus

Online Video Bonus
Watch me create a project schedule on a monthly calendar:
www.TealandLime.com/ProjectHomeBonus

Your completed project schedule tells you two things: when you expect your project to be complete, and when (and by whom) tasks need to be completed in order to meet that date. If your time estimates are relatively accurate and you follow your project schedule, you should be able to complete the project by the last date on your project schedule. If you fall behind on tasks or your estimates are way off, then your timeline will be different. You can revisit the triple constraints to see if reducing scope or adding money to the project can help meet the planned timeline.

Take Action

- Go back to your task notes from the work breakdown exercise and identify task dependencies. What needs to finish before another task can start?
- Once you know the task dependencies, work backwards to find your project starting point. It's the one task most other tasks depend on.
- Figure out the logical sequence for your tasks by drawing a Network Logic Diagram. Pro tip: Use a pencil so you can easily make changes as you work out the best order of events.
- Identify key lead and lag times you might be able to use to your advantage to get ahead on your project timeline.
- Get out the calendar and create your project schedule. Transfer tasks from your Network Logic Diagram onto the calendar where there is enough time and resources to complete the task.

You did it! You completed your project schedule—your day-by-day, play-by-play plan for completing your project. Now that your scope definition, requirements, and project schedule are complete, there's only one other critical project management tool you need: the budget. In the next chapter, you'll learn about the two key activities to do before you prepare your project budget.

CHAPTER ELEVEN

Cost Estimating

Money must be managed. Without a budget, you're constantly guessing and keeping a running (and often inaccurate) tally in your head. Knowing the total amount of money you have to spend on your project is great, but it's not a budget until you break down exactly how you plan to spend the money. Just like the project schedule, you can't jump straight to the budget. To create a budget, you need to do a little pre-work called cost estimating.

A detailed budget is a key tool for tracking project spending. With a budget, you'll know where you overspent, where you underspent, and where you can make up the difference. You need to keep track of your actual costs during the project, as well as important assumptions you make. In this chapter you'll learn how to:

- Estimate project costs so there aren't any disappointing surprises midway through your project.
- Clarify your cost assumptions to increase the likelihood your actual costs will match or be lower than your estimated costs (that means under budget!).

Figuring Out How Much It Will Cost

A project cost estimate is how much you expect the entire project to cost. Just as with time estimates, because we aren't very good at estimating the whole so it's more effective to break cost estimates into smaller parts, estimate them individually, and then total them up.

Most home projects are estimated using a top-down approach. You start with a total projected cost, either a guess or the maximum you want to spend, and then work backwards. A top-down estimate leaves you with very little wiggle room during the project because you're limited by the amount you budgeted for each item (not knowing if it is actually enough to get what you want). Top-down estimates are only good for a sanity check on your total number. If you don't have enough money to allocate to each individual category, then your total number isn't enough.

Top-down Estimate Example
Total master bedroom makeover estimate: $1800
Bed: $800
Bedding: $500
Artwork: $500

A better way to estimate is called bottom-up. It takes more time to put together but will be more realistic. In this approach, you don't start with an end number in mind. You start with a list of expenses. Then you research each expense to come up with an informed cost estimate. At the end, you add up the estimates for each task to get a total cost estimate for the project.

Bottom-up Estimate Example

Bed: Upholstered bed is $795 at Store A, $850 at store B with a 10% discount, shipping at either store is $100, use $865 for estimate.

Bedding: $200 for duvet cover, $100 for sheet set, $150 for decorative pillows, $75 for throw blanket, pick up locally to avoid shipping, use $550 for estimate.

Artwork: Original artwork from local artist is $225 per print, need two prints to go above headboard, pick up locally to avoid shipping, use $450 for estimate.

Total master bedroom makeover estimate: $1865

Because you researched the true costs of each line item in the bottom-up version, you will have more confidence in this estimate. Which is then useful for determining whether you can do the project right now, if you need to save up, or if you want to change the scope.

EIGHT OFTEN OVERLOOKED COSTS

When putting your estimates together, don't forget these eight often overlooked costs:

- **Supplies/Materials** - Include *all* the things you need to buy to get the project done. Don't forget the small things (they add up!). For example, if your project includes tiling, don't forget the grout spacers. If you plan to do landscaping, don't forget the mulch.

- **Tools** - Tool cost is an investment that will be useful for more than one project, but the cost of the tool must fall into the original project for which it's purchased. The benefit is that the cost won't be there for any future project requiring the same tool. If the tool you need is too expensive or you don't plan on using it again in the future, see if you can rent the tool from your local home improvement store or borrow it from a friend or neighbor. I borrowed a miter saw from my dad a couple years ago and I'm still borrowing it. I just found out it's actually my brother's saw that he loaned to my dad. It's a family saw now. No need for all of us to own one.

- **Building Permits and Fees** - For major remodels, additions, and even some outdoor work, you may need building permits, inspections, or to pay other fees. You can usually find these fees on your city or local government website. If you are working with a contractor, be sure to ask them about all the associated fees.

- **Labor** - Include any cost you incur to pay someone to do work on the project (electrical, plumbing, carpenter, etc.). Don't forget tips, where applicable. If you make a deal with your dad to give him a case of beer for helping out, include the beer in your project cost too.

- **Consulting** - Include any cost you incur to pay someone to advise you on your project, like an architect, designer, Feng Shui specialist, etc. Be sure to plan for all the fees associated with their service throughout your project.

- **Shipping/Delivery** - Include the cost of getting supplies and materials to your house or to the project work site. If you plan to order from an online retailer, add the item to your cart to see what the estimated shipping costs are and include that amount in your budget. Pay close attention to special surcharges or delivery fees for bulky or oversized items. Also, consider ordering several things from the same place to get a break on shipping. For example, a furniture store might charge a flat delivery fee whether they bring you one piece of furniture or a whole truck full.

- **Maintenance/Warranty** - This could be on labor or for goods. For complex projects or remodels, it's a good idea to plan for the cost of a warranty or one year of maintenance in the project budget.
- **Taxes** - This is such an easy one to overlook. Make sure to factor in taxes as appropriate for each item. Remember that labor, consulting, and building permits or fees may be taxed as well.

There's just one more step to creating a really good cost estimate.

CHECK YOUR ASSUMPTIONS

The last important step in creating a good cost estimate is to clarify your assumptions, or, better yet, don't make any. Assumptions are things you accept as true, but may not be. Sometimes you may make an assumption without realizing it. If you count on an assumption and it isn't true, your cost estimate might be wrong. If you make assumptions about cost, it's important to note them so you can verify they are true or adjust your estimates if you discover they're not.

Here are four common cost assumptions that most people make. For an honest project budget, you must verify these assumptions:

1. **Sale Price** - You assume you can get a sale price on an item. This assumption is an input to the budget you set for this item. It's important to note this assumption so you remember to buy the item before the

sale ends or know you need to wait for the next sale.

2. **Coupon or Discount** - You assume you can use a coupon or store discount to get a better price on the item. You need to verify that the item is eligible for the coupon or discount. You need to make sure you buy the item before the coupon or discount expires.

3. **Buying in Bulk** - Sometimes you can get a better price on an item if you buy several at once. This works out to your advantage if you need or use a lot of the same item. When I bought baseboard trim for our basement, I noticed a small sticker on the shelf at the home improvement store that said there was a discounted price if I bought ten or more of the same item. Instead of buying a few pieces of baseboard here and there, I calculated how much I needed in total, bought it all at once, and saved 10%. If your budget assumes bulk pricing, you need to make sure you buy the items in bulk. This usually means all the items must be purchased at the same time. If you end up short, you will have to buy the subsequent items at the regular price.

4. **Shopping at a Clearance Center, Outlet, or Discount Retailer** - You assume you can get a better price by shopping around. With this assumption, you should plan for the additional time it might take to find a great deal. Also, understand the risk to your project schedule or scope if you cannot find the item at a bargain price within your required time period.

If you're making any of these cost assumptions, you should note them on your budget (more on that in the next section), so you make sure to hold out for the sale, bring your coupon, buy in bulk, or shop at a discount retailer.

TAKE ACTION

- Create a bottom-up estimate for your most important project. Research each line item to figure out the most likely cost, then add it up to get your total estimated cost. Pro tip: Skip ahead and download the *Project Home* Budget Planner so you can document your cost estimates directly onto your budget.
- Review your cost estimates to make sure you've accounted for the eight often overlooked costs: supplies/materials, tools, building permits and fees, labor, consulting, shipping/delivery, maintenance/ warranty, and taxes.
- Check your cost assumptions. Make sure you can get that sale price, use your coupon or discount, buy in bulk, or find what you need at a clearance center, outlet, or discount retailer. If not, adjust your cost estimate for that item.

You're amazing! Look how far you've made it. There's only one part left to your most successful project plan ever. Estimating costs and checking your assumptions is a good start, but you need a tool for managing your project spending against your estimates. That is what a budget is for. Your project budget is a place to capture and track your cost estimates, but it's also a tool to help you manage costs throughout the project so you can stay on or under budget. In the next chapter, you'll learn how to prepare and use a project budget.

CHAPTER TWELVE

How to Create a Project Budget

You've come so far and your complete project plan is just around the corner. I know two "numbers" chapters in a row is killer, but you've already finished the hard one. Putting your budget together is easy once you have good cost estimates and clarified assumptions. In this chapter, you'll learn how to:

- Fill out your project budget with your cost estimates and then use it to track actual costs.
- Use one simple formula to calculate whether you are on budget, over budget, or under budget. Create a buffer against project risk so you're prepared when something costs more than you expected or an unforeseen cost arises.

CREATING YOUR PROJECT BUDGET

At this point, creating your budget is a matter of transferring your cost estimates to the budget template included in the TAKE ACTION section at the end of this chapter. The budget template includes fields for recording each item needed for your project, your cost estimate, and your assumptions about the cost. You can input all of the data—your cost estimates and assumptions—from the work you did in the last chapter. You'll also notice a few other columns for tracking your actual spending, variance, and contingency. We'll discuss those in the next section.

A budget isn't something you look at once when you create it. If you want to keep your project on budget, it's a tool you need to refer to throughout your project.

Online Bonus

Download the *Project Home* Budget Planner:
www.TealandLime.com/ProjectHomeBonus

More Than Just Numbers

I used to think a budget, whether at work or home, was just a piece of paper with a bunch of numbers on it. I'm not a numbers person. I struggled to see the value in documenting a bunch of numbers in a spreadsheet, until I understood what turns those numbers into a valuable tool. A good budget is so much more than numbers in a spreadsheet. With the right data and calculations, your budget is a thermometer for the health of your project.

I want to introduce you to two new terms that turn your budget into a tool: contingency and variance.

In Case of an Emergency

Contingency is your buffer for risk. Risks are things that could happen, that you don't foresee or can't plan for. Every project has risk. Project risks that come true can cause the project to cost more or take more time to complete. No project runs perfectly, but you can improve the outcome if you're prepared for the unexpected. Contingency is a planned buffer of resources to help absorb some of the impact if a project risk is realized.

The most common place to build in contingency is in the budget. This is the reason for the standard recommendation to add 10-15% to your remodeling budget just in case something goes wrong or costs more than you expect. The larger the project and the greater the risk, the bigger you want to make your contingency budget, just in case. You would only use the contingency for risks that are realized, like mold under the flooring that needs to be cleaned before you can install the new flooring for which you've budgeted.

Contingency = A monetary buffer for risk, usually a percentage of total cost.

If you estimate your project will cost $1000, add 15%, or $150, for contingency. The total budgeted amount will be $1150, where $150 is reserved in case of emergency.

What if you can't afford any extra for contingency? My first suggestion would always be to cut back some scope, so you have a monetary contingency. This is nonnegotiable if you hire a contractor or labor, because they will expect to be paid if it takes longer than they estimated. If you have a very small contingency or no contingency, then you could add a time contingency. That is an extra time buffer in your project schedule, because sometimes extra time can help you save money. For example, instead of paying a landscape crew to install a paver patio, you could do it yourself. It will take longer, but you'll save the labor cost. Just beware that the DIY route isn't always a money-saver and sometimes the extra time required isn't the best trade-off. So, I highly recommend you make sure every project has a monetary buffer against risk.

Your goal is to NOT spend the contingency. It should be used only for unexpected costs arising from risks that come true. It is not extra money to spend on whatever you want. If you use your contingency on something frivolous early on in your project, then you won't have a monetary buffer when a risk turns into a major problem. Think of it like your emergency savings account. You don't dip into it unless something catastrophic goes wrong. The best-run projects finish on time, on or under budget, and don't use any of the planned contingency.

ARE YOU OVER BUDGET OR UNDER BUDGET?

Variance is the budgeted amount (your estimate) minus the actual cost of an item. Said another way, it's what you planned to spend minus what you actually spent. The difference between your estimates and actual costs will reveal if you are on budget or not. If the variance is negative, then you overspent. If it's positive, you're under budget. Each item on your budget will have a variance and the overall project will have a total variance. Variance is key for tracking how well you stick to your budget.

Variance = Budget (Estimate) - Actual

When you overspend it looks like this: $200 (budgeted) - $250 (actual cost) = **-$50**

That's $50 over budget!

When you underspend it looks like this: $200 (budgeted) - $150 (actual cost) = **$50**

That's $50 under budget.

You don't need to stay under budget on every individual

line item. But ideally you will stay on or under budget for your project as a whole. That means keeping your total variance positive. How do you do that? If you overspend on an item, you need to adjust how much you plan to spend on another item to keep the budget in check. If you underspend on an item, you can plan to spend more somewhere else or add the money you saved to your contingency, which is what I recommend.

TAKE ACTION

- Transfer your cost estimates and cost assumptions to the *Project Home* Budget Planner.
- Add contingency to your project budget. Make sure this amount is reasonable for the amount of risk on the project. In general, the larger or more complex the project, the more contingency should be planned.
- Start tracking your spending. Document the actual cost of each item. Calculate the variance for each item and keep an eye on your total variance. Keep it positive!

That's it. Congratulations! Now you're armed with key project management tools—scope definition, schedule, and budget—that will help you manage your triple constraints and have a successful project. With these tools, your most important project will be your most successful project yet!

Conclusion

Building basic project management skills is a must for all homeowners. Every "task" on your to-do list is actually a project. Good project management isn't reserved for large projects or major renovations. Even small projects can benefit from thoughtful project management. If you followed the tips in Part One to improve your project motivation and focus, then all that's left is project planning and follow through so every project you work on is a success. You can do this, and the more often you do, the better you'll get at tackling each of your projects no matter how big or small.

When you put them all together, the strategies in this book will help you go from idea to completion with your next project. Every new idea should be run through the four-step prioritization process in Chapters Four and Five. Once you have a prioritized project list to work from, don't add any new projects. Track new ideas on a separate list and include them in your next planning and prioritization session. At that point you can determine if they should jump the line ahead of other projects.

When you choose your next project, the three critical things to pay attention to are scope, time, and cost, also known as your triple constraints. Remember, the constraints are like a triangle, and your job throughout the project is to keep the triangle balanced, but you can't control all three constraints. Good project management requires making informed trade-offs between the constraints to keep the project on track. The best projects use careful planning upfront to minimize the number of trade-offs that have to be made later.

Start your next project by clearly defining your scope. To stay on track and avoid scope creep, make sure your scope definition states what's in scope and what's out of scope. Scope management starts with your scope definition but continues throughout the project. You must evaluate each change to the project and determine how it impacts not only scope but also your schedule and budget.

Once your scope is clearly defined, create a project schedule. This is more than plotting dates on a calendar. A project schedule requires four key inputs: a work breakdown, time estimates, sequencing, and resources. To create the most realistic timeline for any project, you must identify all the tasks required in order to complete the project and how long you think each task will take. With that information in hand, you can develop a project schedule and determine when your project will most likely be finished.

With a scope definition and project schedule complete, create your project budget. Most people want to start with this step, but if you do, you run the risk of missing important tasks and project needs that will impact the budget. In addition to a clear scope and project timeline, there are two additional inputs to the project budget: cost estimates and assumptions. The most accurate budget requires a little extra planning, but it pays off in the end.

Together your scope definition, project schedule, and project budget are your most important tools for managing a successful project and getting it done. Once created, these tools serve as roadmaps and checkpoints along the way. You will have a better chance of completing a successful project if you follow the map you created and check in frequently to make sure you're on the right path.

Whether you realize it or not, you are a project manager. The success of every item on your to-do list is in your hands. Remember, most projects fail because they never get started, they fizzle out somewhere in the middle and never get finished, or they don't meet expectations when they're done. Armed with the skills you learned in this book, your projects will be different. Feel confident in your ability to choose the right projects, maintain your momentum, adjust for unforeseen obstacles that might occur, and finish strong. You can do this!

MORE BOOKS IN THE
DECORATOR'S FIELD GUIDE SERIES

How To Shop Smart, Save Money, and Love Your Home Decor

Free Decorating is a strategy that could save you tens of thousands of dollars over the life of your home. In *Free Decorating*, you'll learn how to:

- Stop over-spending on the wrong things
- Identify what you really love before you buy
- Build up your *Free Decorating* decor collection
- Re-style any space for free

Can you afford to keep buying (and replacing) the wrong things for your home? Or are you ready to find the decor with staying power?

www.tealandlime.com/books

ACKNOWLEDGEMENTS

This book would not have been possible without the amazing support of my family and friends. Thank you:

José, Pepé, and Jax for being my super fans. I do the projects I do in our home because I want to make it the best possible place for you. Thank you for giving me the time and support to write this book so I can help other moms create a beautiful home for their families.

Mom and Dad for introducing me to home improvement projects and later helping us with several of our own.

Jess, Dan, Andy, Andrea, Jackie, Petra, Terri, Karen, Jane, and Jessica for your encouragement and feedback throughout the writing process.

Kelsey, my graphic designer, and Janna, my editor, for making this book look and read better than I ever could have on my own.

About the Author

Jackie Hernandez is a self-taught professional decorator that believes there is a decorator inside everyone. It is her passion and calling to help women discover their inner decorator and gain the confidence to make their home a beautiful reflection of themselves. Through her own self-discovery and work with over 250 clients and students, Jackie knows the real skills you need to decorate your own home.

Jackie helps the style-confused and decorating-challenged by making interior design simple, practical, and fun. Her straightforward, relatable decorating tips and how to's are helping everyday women confidently decorate their homes and learn more about themselves in the process. Jackie shares free weekly decorating advice on her blog at www.TealandLime.com.

In 2014, Jackie founded School of Decorating (www.SchoolofDecorating.com) where she teaches in-depth, online decorating classes to help you decorate your entire home. School of Decorating (also known as SoD) is a place to learn, connect, and grow with other real women, decorating real homes. In addition to a library of decorating classes, teaching the science behind the art, SoD is a community of decorate-it-yourselfers sharing inspiration, support, and encouragement.

With a Bachelor's of Science in Biology from Michigan Tech University, as a United States Air Force Veteran, and a former professional project manager and Information Technology manager, Jackie brings a diverse set of skills and unique perspective to the decorating world—a mix of science, order, and creativity. You might say she specializes in explaining really complex concepts in easy to understand ways.

Decorating and home design have always been a personal interest. Jackie's favorite childhood pastime was drawing floor plans for dream houses. Her favorite gifts were graph paper, pencils, rulers, and the furniture drafting stencils her dad gave her that she now shares with her son.

With her husband, Jackie has owned and decorated three homes: a tri-level condo with the living room and kitchen on the third floor overlooking the Chesapeake Bay in Virginia, a split-level "builder basic" townhouse in Minnesota, and their current single-family suburban "dream home" near St. Paul, MN.

When she's not "helping other mommies decorate," as her boys describe her work, you can find Jackie life-hacking and experimenting in her home, reading non-fiction books, and spending family time with her husband, two boys, and two border collies.

CONNECT WITH JACKIE:

Blog:
www.tealandlime.com

Classes:
www.schoolofdecorating.com

Facebook:
www.facebook.com/tealandlime

Instagram:
www.instagram.com/tealandlime

Twitter:
www.twitter.com/tealandlime

More books in the Decorator's Field Guide series:
www.tealandlime.com/books

1. Tropical Dusk
   Burnt Russet
   Oxford White

2. Knitting Needles
   Gray Clouds

MS
1800 W
14.5 amp
32.4 lb.

Made in the USA
Lexington, KY
14 May 2018